On
Managing People

HBR'S
10
MUST
READS

On Managing People

HARVARD BUSINESS REVIEW PRESS
Boston, Massachusetts

Library of Congress Cataloging-in-Publication Data

HBR's 10 must reads on managing people.

    p. cm.

  Includes index.

   ISBN 978-1-4221-5801-2 (pbk. : alk. paper) 1. Supervision of employees. 2. Management. 3. Personnel management. I. Harvard business review. II. Title: HBR's ten must reads on managing people. III. Title: Harvard Business review's 10 must reads on managing people.

  HF5549.12.H395 2010

  658.3—dc22

                                         2010031618

Contents

On
Managing People

Leadership That Gets Results

by Daniel Goleman

ASK ANY GROUP OF businesspeople the question "What do effective leaders do?" and you'll hear a sweep of answers. Leaders set strategy; they motivate; they create a mission; they build a culture. Then ask "What *should* leaders do?" If the group is seasoned, you'll likely hear one response: the leader's singular job is to get results.

But how? The mystery of what leaders can and ought to do in order to spark the best performance from their people is age-old. In recent years, that mystery has spawned an entire cottage industry: literally thousands of "leadership experts" have made careers of testing and coaching executives, all in pursuit of creating businesspeople who can turn bold objectives—be they strategic, financial, organizational, or all three—into reality.

Still, effective leadership eludes many people and organizations. One reason is that until recently, virtually no quantitative research has demonstrated which precise leadership behaviors yield positive results. Leadership experts proffer advice based on inference, experience, and instinct. Sometimes that advice is which precise leadership behaviors yield positive results. Leadership experts proffer advice based on inference, experience, and instinct. Sometimes that advice is right on target; sometimes it's not.

But new research by the consulting firm Hay/McBer, which draws on a random sample of 3,871 executives selected from a database of more than 20,000 executives worldwide, takes much of the mystery out of effective leadership. The research found six distinct leadership styles, each springing from different components of emotional intelligence. The styles, taken individually, appear to have a direct and unique impact on the working atmosphere of a company, division, or team, and in turn, on its financial performance. And perhaps most important, the research indicates that leaders with the best results do not rely on only one leadership style; they use most of them in a given week—seamlessly and in different measure—depending on the business situation. Imagine the styles, then, as the array of clubs in a golf pro's bag. Over the course of a game, the pro picks and chooses clubs based on the demands of the shot. Sometimes he has to ponder his selection, but usually it is automatic. The pro senses the challenge ahead, swiftly pulls out the right tool, and elegantly puts it to work. That's how high-impact leaders operate, too.

What are the six styles of leadership? None will shock workplace veterans. Indeed, each style, by name and brief description alone, will likely resonate with anyone who leads, is led, or as is the case with most of us, does both. *Coercive leaders* demand immediate compliance. *Authoritative leaders* mobilize people toward a vision. *Affiliative leaders* create emotional bonds and harmony. *Democratic leaders* build consensus through participation. *Pacesetting leaders* expect excellence and self-direction. And *coaching leaders* develop people for the future.

Close your eyes and you can surely imagine a colleague who uses any one of these styles. You most likely use at least one yourself. What is new in this research, then, is its implications for action. First, it offers a fine-grained understanding of how different leadership styles affect performance and results. Second, it offers clear guidance on when a manager should switch between them. It also strongly suggests that switching flexibly is well advised. New, too, is the research's finding that each leadership style springs from different components of emotional intelligence.

Idea in Brief

Many managers mistakenly assume that leadership style is a function of personality rather than strategic choice. Instead of choosing the one style that suits their temperament, they should ask which style best addresses the demands of a particular situation.

Research has shown that the most successful leaders have strengths in the following emotional intelligence competencies: **self-awareness, self-regulation, motivation, empathy, and social skill**. There are six basic styles of leadership; each makes use of the key components of emotional intelligence in different combinations. The best leaders don't know just one style of leadership—they're skilled at several, and have the flexibility to switch between styles as the circumstances dictate.

Measuring Leadership's Impact

It has been more than a decade since research first linked aspects of emotional intelligence to business results. The late David McClelland, a noted Harvard University psychologist, found that leaders with strengths in a critical mass of six or more emotional intelligence competencies were far more effective than peers who lacked such strengths. For instance, when he analyzed the performance of division heads at a global food and beverage company, he found that among leaders with this critical mass of competence, 87% placed in the top third for annual salary bonuses based on their business performance. More telling, their divisions on average outperformed yearly revenue targets by 15% to 20%. Those executives who lacked emotional intelligence were rarely rated as outstanding in their annual performance reviews, and their divisions underperformed by an average of almost 20%.

Our research set out to gain a more molecular view of the links among leadership and emotional intelligence, and climate and performance. A team of McClelland's colleagues headed by Mary Fontaine and Ruth Jacobs from Hay/McBer studied data about or observed thousands of executives, noting specific behaviors and their impact on climate.[1] How did each individual motivate direct reports? Manage change initiatives? Handle crises? It was in a later phase of

Idea in Practice

Managers often fail to appreciate how profoundly the organizational climate can influence financial results. It can account for nearly a third of financial performance. Organizational climate, in turn, is influenced by leadership style—by the way that managers motivate direct reports, gather and use information, make decisions, manage change initiatives, and handle crises. There are six basic leadership styles. Each derives from different emotional intelligence competencies, works best in particular situations, and affects the organizational climate in different ways.

1. **The coercive style.** This "Do what I say" approach can be very effective in a turnaround situation, a natural disaster, or when working with problem employees. But in most situations, coercive leadership inhibits the organization's flexibility and dampens employees' motivation.

2. **The authoritative style.** An authoritative leader takes a "Come with me" approach: she states the overall goal but gives people the freedom to choose their own means of achieving it. This style works especially well when a business is adrift. It is less effective when the leader is working with a team of experts who are more experienced than he is.

3. **The affiliative style.** The hallmark of the affiliative leader is a "People come first" attitude. This style is particularly useful for building team harmony or increasing morale. But its exclusive focus on praise can

the research that we identified which emotional intelligence capabilities drive the six leadership styles. How does he rate in terms of self-control and social skill? Does a leader show high or low levels of empathy?

The team tested each executive's immediate sphere of influence for its climate. "Climate" is not an amorphous term. First defined by psychologists George Litwin and Richard Stringer and later refined by McClelland and his colleagues, it refers to six key factors that influence an organization's working environment: its *flexibility*—that is, how free employees feel to innovate unencumbered by red tape; their sense of *responsibility* to the organization; the level of *standards* that people set; the sense of accuracy about performance allow poor performance to go uncorrected. Also, affiliative leaders rarely offer advice, which often leaves employees in a quandary.

4. **The democratic style.** This style's impact on organizational climate is not as high as you might imagine. By giving workers a voice in decisions, democratic leaders build organizational flexibility and responsibility and help generate fresh ideas. But sometimes the price is endless meetings and confused employees who feel leaderless.

5. **The pacesetting style.** A leader who sets high performance standards and exemplifies them himself has a very positive impact on employees who are self-motivated and highly competent. But other employees tend to feel overwhelmed by such a leader's demands for excellence—and to resent his tendency to take over a situation.

6. **The coaching style.** This style focuses more on personal development than on immediate work-related tasks. It works well when employees are already aware of their weaknesses and want to improve, but not when they are resistant to changing their ways.

The more styles a leader has mastered, the better. In particular, being able to switch among the authoritative, affiliative, democratic, and coaching styles as conditions dictate creates the best organizational climate and optimizes business performance.

feedback and aptness of *rewards*; the *clarity* people have about mission and values; and finally, the level of *commitment* to a common purpose.

We found that all six leadership styles have a measurable effect on each aspect of climate. (For details, see "Getting Molecular: The Impact of Leadership Styles on Drivers of Climate.") Further, when we looked at the impact of climate on financial results—such as return on sales, revenue growth, efficiency, and profitability—we found a direct correlation between the two. Leaders who used styles that positively affected the climate had decidedly better financial results than those who did not. That is not to say that organizational climate is the only driver of performance. Economic conditions and competitive dynamics matter enormously. But our analysis strongly suggests that climate accounts for nearly a third of results. And that's simply too much of an impact to ignore.

The Styles in Detail

Executives use six leadership styles, but only four of the six consistently have a positive effect on climate and results. Let's look then at each style of leadership in detail. (For a summary of the material that follows, see the chart "The Six Leadership Styles at a Glance.")

The coercive style

The computer company was in crisis mode—its sales and profits were falling, its stock was losing value precipitously, and its shareholders were in an uproar. The board brought in a new CEO with a reputation as a turnaround artist. He set to work chopping jobs, selling off divisions, and making the tough decisions that should have been executed years before. The company was saved, at least in the short-term.

From the start, though, the CEO created a reign of terror, bullying and demeaning his executives, roaring his displeasure at the slightest misstep. The company's top echelons were decimated not just by his erratic firings but also by defections. The CEO's direct reports, frightened by his tendency to blame the bearer of bad news, stopped bringing him any news at all. Morale was at an all-time low—a fact reflected in another downturn in the business after the short-term recovery. The CEO was eventually fired by the board of directors.

It's easy to understand why of all the leadership styles, the coercive one is the least effective in most situations. Consider what the style does to an organization's climate. Flexibility is the hardest hit. The leader's extreme top-down decision making kills new ideas on the vine. People feel so disrespected that they think, "I won't even bring my ideas up—they'll only be shot down." Likewise, people's sense of responsibility evaporates: unable to act on their own initiative, they lose their sense of ownership and feel little accountability for their performance. Some become so resentful they adopt the attitude, "I'm not going to help this bastard."

Coercive leadership also has a damaging effect on the rewards system. Most high-performing workers are motivated by more than money—they seek the satisfaction of work well done. The coercive style erodes such pride. And finally, the style undermines one of the leader's prime tools—motivating people by showing them how their job fits into a grand, shared mission. Such a loss, measured in terms of diminished clarity and commitment, leaves people alienated from their own jobs, wondering, "How does any of this matter?"

Given the impact of the coercive style, you might assume it should never be applied. Our research, however, uncovered a few occasions when it worked masterfully. Take the case of a division president who was brought in to change the direction of a food company that was losing money. His first act was to have the executive conference room demolished. To him, the room—with its long marble table that looked like "the deck of the Starship Enterprise"—symbolized the tradition-bound formality that was paralyzing the company. The destruction of the room, and the subsequent move to a smaller, more informal setting, sent a message no one could miss, and the division's culture changed quickly in its wake.

That said, the coercive style should be used only with extreme caution and in the few situations when it is absolutely imperative, such as during a turnaround or when a hostile takeover is looming. In those cases, the coercive style can break failed business habits and shock people into new ways of working. It is always appropriate during a genuine emergency, like in the aftermath of an earthquake or a fire. And it can work with problem employees with whom all else has failed. But if a leader relies solely on this style or continues to use it once the emergency passes, the long-term impact of his insensitivity to the morale and feelings of those he leads will be ruinous.

The authoritative style

Tom was the vice president of marketing at a floundering national restaurant chain that specialized in pizza. Needless to say, the company's poor performance troubled the senior managers, but they were at a loss for what to do. Every Monday, they met to review

Emotional Intelligence: A Primer

Emotional intelligence—the ability to manage ourselves and our relationships effectively—consists of four fundamental capabilities: self-awareness, self-management, social awareness, and social skill. Each capability, in turn, is composed of specific sets of competencies. Below is a list of the capabilities and their corresponding traits.

Self-Awareness

- *Emotional self-awareness:* the ability to read and understand your emotions as well as recognize their impact on work performance, relationships, and the like.

- *Accurate self-assessment:* a realistic evaluation of your strengths and limitations.

- *Self-confidence:* a strong and positive sense of self-worth.

Self-Management

- *Self-control:* the ability to keep disruptive emotions and impulses under control.

- *Trustworthiness:* a consistent display of honesty and integrity.

- *Conscientiousness:* the ability to manage yourself and your responsibilities.

- *Adaptability:* skill at adjusting to changing situations and overcoming obstacles.

- *Achievement orientation:* the drive to meet an internal standard of excellence.

- *Initiative:* a readiness to seize opportunities.

recent sales, struggling to come up with fixes. To Tom, the approach didn't make sense. "We were always trying to figure out why our sales were down last week. We had the whole company looking backward instead of figuring out what we had to do tomorrow."

Tom saw an opportunity to change people's way of thinking at an off-site strategy meeting. There, the conversation began with stale truisms: the company had to drive up shareholder wealth and increase return on assets. Tom believed those concepts didn't have the

Social Awareness

- *Empathy:* skill at sensing other people's emotions, understanding their perspective, and taking an active interest in their concerns.

- *Organizational awareness:* the ability to read the currents of organizational life, build decision networks, and navigate politics.

- *Service orientation:* the ability to recognize and meet customers' needs.

Social Skill

- *Visionary leadership:* the ability to take charge and inspire with a compelling vision.

- *Influence:* the ability to wield a range of persuasive tactics.

- *Developing others:* the propensity to bolster the abilities of others through feedback and guidance.

- *Communication:* skill at listening and at sending clear, convincing, and well-tuned messages.

- *Change catalyst:* proficiency in initiating new ideas and leading people in a new direction.

- *Conflict management:* the ability to de-escalate disagreements and orchestrate resolutions.

- *Building bonds:* proficiency at cultivating and maintaining a web of relationships.

- *Teamwork and collaboration:* competence at promoting cooperation and building teams.

power to inspire a restaurant manager to be innovative or to do better than a good-enough job.

So Tom made a bold move. In the middle of a meeting, he made an impassioned plea for his colleagues to think from the customer's perspective. Customers want convenience, he said. The company was not in the restaurant business, it was in the business of distributing high-quality, convenient-to-get pizza. That notion—and nothing else—should drive everything the company did.

Getting Molecular: The Impact of Leadership Styles on Drivers of Climate

Our research investigated how each leadership style affected the six drivers of climate, or working atmosphere. The figures below show the correlation between each leadership style and each aspect of climate. So, for instance, if we look at the climate driver of flexibility, we see that the coercive style has a $-.28$ correlation while the democratic style has a .28 correlation, equally strong in the opposite direction. Focusing on the authoritative leadership style, we find that it has a .54 correlation with rewards—strongly positive—and a .21 correlation with responsibility—positive, but not as strong. In other words, the style's correlation with rewards was more than twice that with responsibility.

According to the data, the authoritative leadership style has the most positive effect on climate, but three others—affiliative, democratic, and coaching—follow close behind. That said, the research indicates that no style should be relied on exclusively, and all have at least short-term uses.

	Coercive	Authoritative	Affiliative	Democratic	Pacesetting	Coaching
Flexibility	$-.28$	.32	.27	.28	$-.07$	.17
Responsibility	$-.37$	.21	.16	.23	.04	.08
Standards	.02	.38	.31	.22	$-.27$	.39
Rewards	$-.18$	.54	.48	.42	$-.29$	.43
Clarity	$-.11$	.44	.37	.35	$-.28$	.38
Commitment	$-.13$	.35	.34	.26	$-.20$	.27
Overall impact on climate	$-.26$	.54	.46	.43	$-.25$	.42

With his vibrant enthusiasm and clear vision—the hallmarks of the authoritative style—Tom filled a leadership vacuum at the company. Indeed, his concept became the core of the new mission statement. But this conceptual breakthrough was just the beginning. Tom made sure that the mission statement was built into the company's strategic planning process as the designated driver of growth. And he ensured that the vision was articulated so that local restaurant managers understood they were the key to the company's success and were free to find new ways to distribute pizza.

Changes came quickly. Within weeks, many local managers started guaranteeing fast, new delivery times. Even better, they started to act like entrepreneurs, finding ingenious locations to open new branches: kiosks on busy street corners and in bus and train stations, even from carts in airports and hotel lobbies.

Tom's success was no fluke. Our research indicates that of the six leadership styles, the authoritative one is most effective, driving up every aspect of climate. Take clarity. The authoritative leader is a visionary; he motivates people by making clear to them how their work fits into a larger vision for the organization. People who work for such leaders understand that what they do matters and why. Authoritative leadership also maximizes commitment to the organization's goals and strategy. By framing the individual tasks within a grand vision, the authoritative leader defines standards that revolve around that vision. When he gives performance feedback—whether positive or negative—the singular criterion is whether or not that performance furthers the vision. The standards for success are clear to all, as are the rewards. Finally, consider the style's impact on flexibility. An authoritative leader states the end but generally gives people plenty of leeway to devise their own means. Authoritative leaders give people the freedom to innovate, experiment, and take calculated risks.

Because of its positive impact, the authoritative style works well in almost any business situation. But it is particularly effective when a business is adrift. An authoritative leader charts a new course and sells his people on a fresh long-term vision.

The authoritative style, powerful though it may be, will not work in every situation. The approach fails, for instance, when a leader is working with a team of experts or peers who are more experienced than he is; they may see the leader as pompous or out-of-touch. Another limitation: if a manager trying to be authoritative becomes overbearing, he can undermine the egalitarian spirit of an effective team. Yet even with such caveats, leaders would be wise to grab for the authoritative "club" more often than not. It may not guarantee a hole in one, but it certainly helps with the long drive.

The affiliative style

If the coercive leader demands, "Do what I say," and the authoritative urges, "Come with me," the affiliative leader says, "People come first." This leadership style revolves around people—its proponents value individuals and their emotions more than tasks and goals. The affiliative leader strives to keep employees happy and to create harmony among them. He manages by building strong emotional bonds and then reaping the benefits of such an approach, namely fierce loyalty. The style also has a markedly positive effect on communication. People who like one another a lot talk a lot. They share ideas; they share inspiration. And the style drives up flexibility; friends trust one another, allowing habitual innovation and risk taking. Flexibility also rises because the affiliative leader, like a parent who adjusts household rules for a maturing adolescent, doesn't impose unnecessary strictures on how employees get their work done. They give people the freedom to do their job in the way they think is most effective.

As for a sense of recognition and reward for work well done, the affiliative leader offers ample positive feedback. Such feedback has special potency in the workplace because it is all too rare: outside of an annual review, most people usually get no feedback on their day-to-day efforts—or only negative feedback. That makes the affiliative leader's positive words all the more motivating. Finally, affiliative leaders are masters at building a sense of belonging. They are, for instance, likely to take their direct reports out for a meal or a drink, one-on-one, to see how they're doing. They will bring in a cake to celebrate a group accomplishment. They are natural relationship builders.

Joe Torre, the heart and soul of the New York Yankees, is a classic affiliative leader. During the 1999 World Series, Torre tended ably to the psyches of his players as they endured the emotional pressure cooker of a pennant race. All season long, he made a special point to praise Scott Brosius, whose father had died during the season, for staying committed even as he mourned. At the celebration party after the team's final game, Torre specifically sought out right fielder Paul O'Neill. Although he had received the news of his father's death that morning, O'Neill chose to play in the decisive game—and he burst into tears the moment it ended. Torre made a point of acknowledging O'Neill's personal struggle, calling him a "warrior." Torre also used the spotlight of the victory celebration to praise two players whose return the following year was threatened by contract disputes. In doing so, he sent a clear message to the team and to the club's owner that he valued the players immensely—too much to lose them.

Along with ministering to the emotions of his people, an affiliative leader may also tend to his own emotions openly. The year Torre's brother was near death awaiting a heart transplant, he shared his worries with his players. He also spoke candidly with the team about his treatment for prostate cancer.

The affiliative style's generally positive impact makes it a good all-weather approach, but leaders should employ it particularly when trying to build team harmony, increase morale, improve communication, or repair broken trust. For instance, one executive in our study was hired to replace a ruthless team leader. The former leader had taken credit for his employees' work and had attempted to pit them against one another. His efforts ultimately failed, but the team he left behind was suspicious and weary. The new executive managed to mend the situation by unstintingly showing emotional honesty and rebuilding ties. Several months in, her leadership had created a renewed sense of commitment and energy.

Despite its benefits, the affiliative style should not be used alone. Its exclusive focus on praise can allow poor performance to go uncorrected; employees may perceive that mediocrity is tolerated. And because affiliative leaders rarely offer constructive advice on how to improve, employees must figure out how to do so on their own. When people need clear directives to navigate through complex challenges, the affiliative style leaves them rudderless. Indeed, if overly relied on, this style can actually steer a group to failure. Perhaps that is why many affiliative leaders, including Torre, use this style in close conjunction with the authoritative style. Authoritative leaders state a vision, set standards, and let people know how their

---

The Six Leadership Styles at a Glance

Our research found that leaders use six styles, each springing from different components of emotional intelligence. Here is a summary of the styles, their origin, when they work best, and their impact on an organization's climate and thus its performance.

	Coercive	Authoritative
The leader's modus operandi	Demands immediate compliance	Mobilizes people toward a vision
The style in a phrase	"Do what I tell you."	"Come with me."
Underlying emotional intelligence competencies	Drive to achieve, initiative, self-control	Self-confidence, empathy, change catalyst
When the style works best	In a crisis, to kick start a turnaround, or with problem employees	When changes require a new vision, or when a clear direction is needed
Overall impact on climate	Negative	Most strongly positive

work is furthering the group's goals. Alternate that with the caring, nurturing approach of the affiliative leader, and you have a potent combination.

The democratic style

Sister Mary ran a Catholic school system in a large metropolitan area. One of the schools—the only private school in an impoverished neighborhood—had been losing money for years, and the archdiocese could no longer afford to keep it open. When Sister Mary eventually got the order to shut it down, she didn't just lock the doors. She called a meeting of all the teachers and staff at the school and explained to them the details of the financial crisis—the first time anyone working at the school had been included in the business side of the institution. She asked for their ideas on ways to keep the school open and on how to handle the closing, should it come to that. Sister Mary spent much of her time at the meeting just listening.

She did the same at later meetings for school parents and for the community and during a successive series of meetings for the school's teachers and staff. After two months of meetings, the consensus was

Affiliative	Democratic	Pacesetting	Coaching
Creates harmony and builds emotional bonds	Forges consensus through participation	Sets high standards for performance	Develops people for the future
"People come first."	"What do you think?"	"Do as I do, now."	"Try this."
Empathy, building relationships, communication	Collaboration, team leadership, communication	Conscientiousness, drive to achieve, initiative	Developing others, empathy, self-awareness
To heal rifts in a team or to motivate people during stressful circumstances	To build buy-in or consensus, or to get input from valuable employees	To get quick results from a highly motivated and competent team	To help an employee improve performance or develop long-term strengths
Positive	Positive	Negative	Positive

clear: the school would have to close. A plan was made to transfer students to other schools in the Catholic system.

The final outcome was no different than if Sister Mary had gone ahead and closed the school the day she was told to. But by allowing the school's constituents to reach that decision collectively, Sister Mary received none of the backlash that would have accompanied such a move. People mourned the loss of the school, but they understood its inevitability. Virtually no one objected.

Compare that with the experiences of a priest in our research who headed another Catholic school. He, too, was told to shut it down. And he did—by fiat. The result was disastrous: parents filed lawsuits, teachers and parents picketed, and local newspapers ran editorials attacking his decision. It took a year to resolve the disputes before he could finally go ahead and close the school.

Sister Mary exemplifies the democratic style in action—and its benefits. By spending time getting people's ideas and buy-in, a leader builds trust, respect, and commitment. By letting workers themselves have a say in decisions that affect their goals and how they do their work, the democratic leader drives up flexibility and responsibility. And by listening to employees' concerns, the democratic leader learns what to do to keep morale high. Finally, because they have a say in setting their goals and the standards for evaluating success, people operating in a democratic system tend to be very realistic about what can and cannot be accomplished.

However, the democratic style has its drawbacks, which is why its impact on climate is not as high as some of the other styles. One of its more exasperating consequences can be endless meetings where ideas are mulled over, consensus remains elusive, and the only visible result is scheduling more meetings. Some democratic leaders use the style to put off making crucial decisions, hoping that enough thrashing things out will eventually yield a blinding insight. In reality, their people end up feeling confused and leaderless. Such an approach can even escalate conflicts.

When does the style work best? This approach is ideal when a leader is himself uncertain about the best direction to take and needs ideas and guidance from able employees. And even if a leader has a strong vision, the democratic style works well to generate fresh ideas for executing that vision.

The democratic style, of course, makes much less sense when employees are not competent or informed enough to offer sound advice. And it almost goes without saying that building consensus is wrongheaded in times of crisis. Take the case of a CEO whose computer company was severely threatened by changes in the market. He always sought consensus about what to do. As competitors stole customers and customers' needs changed, he kept appointing committees to consider the situation. When the market made a sudden shift because of a new technology, the CEO froze in his tracks. The board replaced him before he could appoint yet another task force to consider the situation. The new CEO, while occasionally democratic and affiliative, relied heavily on the authoritative style, especially in his first months.

The pacesetting style

Like the coercive style, the pacesetting style has its place in the leader's repertory, but it should be used sparingly. That's not what we expected to find. After all, the hallmarks of the pacesetting style sound admirable. The leader sets extremely high performance standards and exemplifies them himself. He is obsessive about doing things better and faster, and he asks the same of everyone around him. He quickly pinpoints poor performers and demands more from them. If they don't rise to the occasion, he replaces them with people who can. You would think such an approach would improve results, but it doesn't.

In fact, the pacesetting style destroys climate. Many employees feel overwhelmed by the pacesetter's demands for excellence, and their morale drops. Guidelines for working may be clear in the leader's head, but she does not state them clearly; she expects people to know what to do and even thinks, "If I have to tell you, you're the wrong person for the job." Work becomes not a matter of doing one's best along a clear course so much as second-guessing what the leader wants. At the same time, people often feel that the pacesetter doesn't trust them to work in their own way or to take initiative. Flexibility and responsibility evaporate; work becomes so task focused and routinized it's boring.

As for rewards, the pacesetter either gives no feedback on how people are doing or jumps in to take over when he thinks they're lagging. And if the leader should leave, people feel directionless—they're so used to "the expert" setting the rules. Finally, commitment dwindles under the regime of a pacesetting leader because people have no sense of how their personal efforts fit into the big picture.

For an example of the pacesetting style, take the case of Sam, a biochemist in R&D at a large pharmaceutical company. Sam's superb technical expertise made him an early star: he was the one everyone turned to when they needed help. Soon he was promoted to head of a team developing a new product. The other scientists on the team were as competent and self-motivated as Sam; his métier as team leader became offering himself as a model of how to do first-class scientific work under tremendous deadline pressure, pitching in when needed. His team completed its task in record time.

But then came a new assignment: Sam was put in charge of R&D for his entire division. As his tasks expanded and he had to articulate a vision, coordinate projects, delegate responsibility, and help develop others, Sam began to slip. Not trusting that his subordinates were as capable as he was, he became a micromanager, obsessed with details and taking over for others when their performance slackened. Instead of trusting them to improve with guidance and development, Sam found himself working nights and weekends after stepping in to take over for the head of a floundering research team. Finally, his own boss suggested, to his relief, that he return to his old job as head of a product development team.

Although Sam faltered, the pacesetting style isn't always a disaster. The approach works well when all employees are self-motivated, highly competent, and need little direction or coordination—for example, it can work for leaders of highly skilled and self-motivated professionals, like R&D groups or legal teams. And, given a talented team to lead, pacesetting does exactly that: gets work done on time or even ahead of schedule. Yet like any leadership style, pacesetting should never be used by itself.

The coaching style

A product unit at a global computer company had seen sales plummet from twice as much as its competitors to only half as much. So Lawrence, the president of the manufacturing division, decided to close the unit and reassign its people and products. Upon hearing the news, James, the head of the doomed unit, decided to go over his boss's head and plead his case to the CEO.

What did Lawrence do? Instead of blowing up at James, he sat down with his rebellious direct report and talked over not just the decision to close the division but also James's future. He explained to James how moving to another division would help him develop new skills. It would make him a better leader and teach him more about the company's business.

Lawrence acted more like a counselor than a traditional boss. He listened to James's concerns and hopes, and he shared his own. He said he believed James had grown stale in his current job; it was, after all, the only place he'd worked in the company. He predicted that James would blossom in a new role.

The conversation then took a practical turn. James had not yet had his meeting with the CEO—the one he had impetuously demanded when he heard of his division's closing. Knowing this—and also knowing that the CEO unwaveringly supported the closing—Lawrence took the time to coach James on how to present his case in that meeting. "You don't get an audience with the CEO very often," he noted, "let's make sure you impress him with your thoughtfulness." He advised James not to plead his personal case but to focus on the business unit: "If he thinks you're in there for your own glory, he'll throw you out faster than you walked through the door." And he urged him to put his ideas in writing; the CEO always appreciated that.

Lawrence's reason for coaching instead of scolding? "James is a good guy, very talented and promising," the executive explained to us, "and I don't want this to derail his career. I want him to stay with the company, I want him to work out, I want him to learn, I want him to benefit and grow. Just because he screwed up doesn't mean he's terrible."

Lawrence's actions illustrate the coaching style par excellence. Coaching leaders help employees identify their unique strengths and weaknesses and tie them to their personal and career aspirations. They encourage employees to establish long-term development goals and help them conceptualize a plan for attaining them. They make agreements with their employees about their role and responsibilities in enacting development plans, and they give plentiful instruction and feedback. Coaching leaders excel at delegating; they give employees challenging assignments, even if that means the tasks won't be accomplished quickly. In other words, these leaders are willing to put up with short-term failure if it furthers long-term learning.

Of the six styles, our research found that the coaching style is used least often. Many leaders told us they don't have the time in this high-pressure economy for the slow and tedious work of teaching people and helping them grow. But after a first session, it takes little or no extra time. Leaders who ignore this style are passing up a powerful tool: its impact on climate and performance are markedly positive.

Admittedly, there is a paradox in coaching's positive effect on business performance because coaching focuses primarily on personal development, not on immediate work-related tasks. Even so, coaching improves results. The reason: it requires constant dialogue, and that dialogue has a way of pushing up every driver of climate. Take flexibility. When an employee knows his boss watches him and cares about what he does, he feels free to experiment. After all, he's sure to get quick and constructive feedback. Similarly, the ongoing dialogue of coaching guarantees that people know what is expected of them and how their work fits into a larger vision or strategy. That affects responsibility and clarity. As for commitment, coaching helps there, too, because the style's implicit message is, "I believe in you, I'm investing in you, and I expect your best efforts." Employees very often rise to that challenge with their heart, mind, and soul.

The coaching style works well in many business situations, but it is perhaps most effective when people on the receiving end are "up for it." For instance, the coaching style works particularly well when employees are already aware of their weaknesses and would like to improve their performance. Similarly, the style works well when employees realize how cultivating new abilities can help them advance. In short, it works best with employees who want to be coached.

By contrast, the coaching style makes little sense when employees, for whatever reason, are resistant to learning or changing their ways. And it flops if the leader lacks the expertise to help the employee along. The fact is, many managers are unfamiliar with or simply inept at coaching, particularly when it comes to giving ongoing performance feedback that motivates rather than creates fear or apathy. Some companies have realized the positive impact of the style and are trying to make it a core competence. At some companies, a significant portion of annual bonuses are tied to an executive's development of his or her direct reports. But many organizations have yet to take full advantage of this leadership style. Although the coaching style may not scream "bottom-line results," it delivers them.

Leaders Need Many Styles

Many studies, including this one, have shown that the more styles a leader exhibits, the better. Leaders who have mastered four or more—especially the authoritative, democratic, affiliative, and coaching styles—have the very best climate and business performance. And the most effective leaders switch flexibly among the leadership styles as needed. Although that may sound daunting, we witnessed it more often than you might guess, at both large corporations and tiny start-ups, by seasoned veterans who could explain exactly how and why they lead and by entrepreneurs who claim to lead by gut alone.

Such leaders don't mechanically match their style to fit a checklist of situations—they are far more fluid. They are exquisitely sensitive to the impact they are having on others and seamlessly adjust their style to get the best results. These are leaders, for example, who can read in the first minutes of conversation that a talented but underperforming employee has been demoralized by an unsympathetic, do-it-the-way-I-tell-you manager and needs to be inspired through a reminder of why her work matters. Or that leader might choose to reenergize the employee by asking her about her dreams and aspirations and finding ways to make her job more challenging. Or that initial conversation might signal that the employee needs an ultimatum: improve or leave.

For an example of fluid leadership in action, consider Joan, the general manager of a major division at a global food and beverage company. Joan was appointed to her job while the division was in a deep crisis. It had not made its profit targets for six years; in the most recent year, it had missed by $50 million. Morale among the top management team was miserable; mistrust and resentments were rampant. Joan's directive from above was clear: turn the division around.

Joan did so with a nimbleness in switching among leadership styles that is rare. From the start, she realized she had a short window to demonstrate effective leadership and to establish rapport and trust. She also knew that she urgently needed to be informed about what was not working, so her first task was to listen to key people.

Her first week on the job she had lunch and dinner meetings with each member of the management team. Joan sought to get each person's understanding of the current situation. But her focus was not so much on learning how each person diagnosed the problem as on getting to know each manager as a person. Here Joan employed the affiliative style: she explored their lives, dreams, and aspirations.

She also stepped into the coaching role, looking for ways she could help the team members achieve what they wanted in their careers. For instance, one manager who had been getting feedback that he was a poor team player confided his worries to her. He thought he was a good team member, but he was plagued by persistent complaints. Recognizing that he was a talented executive and a valuable asset to the company, Joan made an agreement with him to point out (in private) when his actions undermined his goal of being seen as a team player.

She followed the one-on-one conversations with a three-day off-site meeting. Her goal here was team building, so that everyone would own whatever solution for the business problems emerged. Her initial stance at the off-site meeting was that of a democratic leader. She encouraged everyone to express freely their frustrations and complaints.

The next day, Joan had the group focus on solutions: each person made three specific proposals about what needed to be done. As Joan clustered the suggestions, a natural consensus emerged about priorities for the business, such as cutting costs. As the group came up with specific action plans, Joan got the commitment and buy-in she sought.

With that vision in place, Joan shifted into the authoritative style, assigning accountability for each follow-up step to specific executives and holding them responsible for their accomplishment. For example, the division had been dropping prices on products without increasing its volume. One obvious solution was to raise prices, but the previous VP of sales had dithered and had let the problem fester. The new VP of sales now had responsibility to adjust the price points to fix the problem.

Over the following months, Joan's main stance was authoritative. She continually articulated the group's new vision in a way that reminded each member of how his or her role was crucial to achieving these goals. And, especially during the first few weeks of the plan's implementation, Joan felt that the urgency of the business crisis justified an occasional shift into the coercive style should someone fail to meet his or her responsibility. As she put it, "I had to be brutal about this follow-up and make sure this stuff happened. It was going to take discipline and focus."

The results? Every aspect of climate improved. People were innovating. They were talking about the division's vision and crowing about their commitment to new, clear goals. The ultimate proof of Joan's fluid leadership style is written in black ink: after only seven months, her division exceeded its yearly profit target by $5 million.

Expanding Your Repertory

Few leaders, of course, have all six styles in their repertory, and even fewer know when and how to use them. In fact, as we have brought the findings of our research into many organizations, the most common responses have been, "But I have only two of those!" and, "I can't use all those styles. It wouldn't be natural."

Such feelings are understandable, and in some cases, the antidote is relatively simple. The leader can build a team with members who employ styles she lacks. Take the case of a VP for manufacturing. She successfully ran a global factory system largely by using the affiliative style. She was on the road constantly, meeting with plant managers, attending to their pressing concerns, and letting them know how much she cared about them personally. She left the division's strategy—extreme efficiency—to a trusted lieutenant with a keen understanding of technology, and she delegated its performance standards to a colleague who was adept at the authoritative approach. She also had a pacesetter on her team who always visited the plants with her.

An alternative approach, and one I would recommend more, is for leaders to expand their own style repertories. To do so, leaders must

Growing Your Emotional Intelligence

Unlike IQ, which is largely genetic—it changes little from childhood—the skills of emotional intelligence can be learned at any age. It's not easy, however. Growing your emotional intelligence takes practice and commitment. But the payoffs are well worth the investment.

Consider the case of a marketing director for a division of a global food company. Jack, as I'll call him, was a classic pacesetter: high-energy, always striving to find better ways to get things done, and too eager to step in and take over when, say, someone seemed about to miss a deadline. Worse, Jack was prone to pounce on anyone who didn't seem to meet his standards, flying off the handle if a person merely deviated from completing a job in the order Jack thought best.

Jack's leadership style had a predictably disastrous impact on climate and business results. After two years of stagnant performance, Jack's boss suggested he seek out a coach. Jack wasn't pleased but, realizing his own job was on the line, he complied.

The coach, an expert in teaching people how to increase their emotional intelligence, began with a 360-degree evaluation of Jack. A diagnosis from multiple viewpoints is essential in improving emotional intelligence because those who need the most help usually have blind spots. In fact, our research found that top-performing leaders overestimate their strengths on, at most, one emotional intelligence ability, whereas poor performers overrate themselves on four or more. Jack was not that far off, but he did rate himself more glowingly than his direct reports, who gave him especially low grades on emotional self-control and empathy.

Initially, Jack had some trouble accepting the feedback data. But when his coach showed him how those weaknesses were tied to his inability to display leadership styles dependent on those competencies—especially the authoritative, affiliative, and coaching styles—Jack realized he had to improve if he wanted to advance in the company. Making such a connection is essential. The reason: improving emotional intelligence isn't done in a weekend or during a seminar—it takes diligent practice on the job, over several months. If people do not see the value of the change, they will not make that effort.

Once Jack zeroed in on areas for improvement and committed himself to making the effort, he and his coach worked up a plan to turn his day-to-day job into a learning laboratory. For instance, Jack discovered he was empathetic when things were calm, but in a crisis, he tuned out others. This tendency hampered his ability to listen to what people were telling him in the very moments he most needed to do so. Jack's plan required him to focus on his behavior during tough situations. As soon as he felt himself tensing up, his job was to immediately step back, let the other person speak, and then ask clarifying questions. The point was to not act judgmental or hostile under pressure.

The change didn't come easily, but with practice Jack learned to defuse his flare-ups by entering into a dialogue instead of launching a harangue. Although he didn't always agree with them, at least he gave people a chance to make their case. At the same time, Jack also practiced giving his direct reports more positive feedback and reminding them of how their work contributed to the group's mission. And he restrained himself from micromanaging them.

Jack met with his coach every week or two to review his progress and get advice on specific problems. For instance, occasionally Jack would find himself falling back on his old pacesetting tactics—cutting people off, jumping in to take over, and blowing up in a rage. Almost immediately, he would regret it. So he and his coach dissected those relapses to figure out what triggered the old ways and what to do the next time a similar moment arose. Such "relapse prevention" measures inoculate people against future lapses or just giving up. Over a six-month period, Jack made real improvement. His own records showed he had reduced the number of flare-ups from one or more a day at the beginning to just one or two a month. The climate had improved sharply, and the division's numbers were starting to creep upward.

Why does improving an emotional intelligence competence take months rather than days? Because the emotional centers of the brain, not just the neocortex, are involved. The neocortex, the thinking brain that learns technical skills and purely cognitive abilities, gains knowledge very quickly, but the emotional brain does not. To master a new behavior, the emotional centers need repetition and practice. Improving your emotional intelligence, then, is akin to changing your habits. Brain circuits that carry leadership habits have to unlearn the old ones and replace them with the new. The more often a behavioral sequence is repeated, the stronger the underlying brain circuits become. At some point, the new neural pathways become the brain's default option. When that happened, Jack was able to go through the paces of leadership effortlessly, using styles that worked for him—and the whole company.

first understand which emotional intelligence competencies underlie the leadership styles they are lacking. They can then work assid-
uously to increase their quotient of them.

For instance, an affiliative leader has strengths in three emotional
intelligence competencies: in empathy, in building relationships,
and in communication. Empathy—sensing how people are feeling in
the moment—allows the affiliative leader to respond to employees
in a way that is highly congruent with that person's emotions, thus
building rapport. The affiliative leader also displays a natural ease in
forming new relationships, getting to know someone as a person,
and cultivating a bond. Finally, the outstanding affiliative leader has
mastered the art of interpersonal communication, particularly in
saying just the right thing or making the apt symbolic gesture at just
the right moment.

So if you are primarily a pacesetting leader who wants to be able
to use the affiliative style more often, you would need to improve
your level of empathy and, perhaps, your skills at building relationships or communicating effectively. As another example, an
authoritative leader who wants to add the democratic style to his
repertory might need to work on the capabilities of collaboration
and communication. Such advice about adding capabilities may
seem simplistic—"Go change yourself"—but enhancing emotional
intelligence is entirely possible with practice. (For more on how to
improve emotional intelligence, see the sidebar "Growing Your
Emotional Intelligence.")

More Science, Less Art

Like parenthood, leadership will never be an exact science. But neither should it be a complete mystery to those who practice it. In recent years, research has helped parents understand the genetic,
psychological, and behavioral components that affect their "job performance." With our new research, leaders, too, can get a clearer picture of what it takes to lead effectively. And perhaps as important,
they can see how they can make that happen.

The business environment is continually changing, and a leader must respond in kind. Hour to hour, day to day, week to week, executives must play their leadership styles like a pro—using the right one at just the right time and in the right measure. The payoff is in the results.

Originally published in March 2000. Reprint R00204.

Notes
1. Daniel Goleman consults with Hay/McBer on leadership development.

One More Time

How Do You Motivate Employees?

by Frederick Herzberg

HOW MANY ARTICLES, BOOKS, speeches, and workshops have pleaded plaintively, "How do I get an employee to do what I want?"

The psychology of motivation is tremendously complex, and what has been unraveled with any degree of assurance is small indeed. But the dismal ratio of knowledge to speculation has not dampened the enthusiasm for new forms of snake oil that are constantly coming on the market, many of them with academic testimonials. Doubtless this article will have no depressing impact on the market for snake oil, but since the ideas expressed in it have been tested in many corporations and other organizations, it will help— I hope—to redress the imbalance in the aforementioned ratio.

"Motivating" with KITA

In lectures to industry on the problem, I have found that the audiences are usually anxious for quick and practical answers, so I will begin with a straightforward, practical formula for moving people.

What is the simplest, surest, and most direct way of getting someone to do something? Ask? But if the person responds that he or she does not want to do it, then that calls for psychological consultation to determine the reason for such obstinacy. Tell the person? The response shows that he or she does not understand you, and now an expert in communication methods has to be brought in to show you how to get through. Give the person a monetary incentive? I do not need to remind the reader of the complexity and difficulty involved in setting up and administering an incentive system. Show the person? This means a costly training program. We need a simple way.

Every audience contains the "direct action" manager who shouts, "Kick the person!" And this type of manager is right. The surest and least circumlocuted way of getting someone to do something is to administer a kick in the pants—to give what might be called the KITA.

There are various forms of KITA, and here are some of them:

Negative physical KITA

This is a literal application of the term and was frequently used in the past. It has, however, three major drawbacks: 1) It is inelegant; 2) it contradicts the precious image of benevolence that most organizations cherish; and 3) since it is a physical attack, it directly stimulates the autonomic nervous system, and this often results in negative feedback—the employee may just kick you in return. These factors give rise to certain taboos against negative physical KITA.

In uncovering infinite sources of psychological vulnerabilities and the appropriate methods to play tunes on them, psychologists have come to the rescue of those who are no longer permitted to use negative physical KITA. "He took my rug away"; "I wonder what she meant by that"; "The boss is always going around me"—these symptomatic expressions of ego sores that have been rubbed raw are the result of application of:

Negative psychological KITA

This has several advantages over negative physical KITA. First, the cruelty is not visible; the bleeding is internal and comes much later. Second, since it affects the higher cortical centers of the brain with its inhibitory powers, it reduces the possibility of physical backlash. Third, since the number of psychological pains that a person can feel

Idea in Brief

Imagine your workforce so motivated that employees relish *more* hours of work, not fewer, initiate increased responsibility themselves, and boast about their challenging work, not their paychecks or bonuses.

An impossible dream? Not if you understand the counterintuitive force behind motivation—and the ineffectiveness of most performance incentives. Despite media attention to the contrary, motivation does *not* come from perks, plush offices, or even promotions or pay. These **extrinsic incentives** may stimulate people to put their noses to the grindstone—but they'll likely perform only as long as it takes to get that next raise or promotion.

The truth? You and your organization have only limited power to motivate employees. Yes, unfair salaries may damage morale. But when you *do* offer fat paychecks and other extrinsic incentives, people *won't* necessarily work harder or smarter.

Why? Most of us are motivated by **intrinsic rewards**: interesting, challenging work, and the opportunity to achieve and grow into greater responsibility.

Of course, you have to provide some extrinsic incentives. After all, few of us can afford to work for *no* salary. But the *real* key to motivating your employees is enabling them to activate their own *internal* generators. Otherwise, you'll be stuck trying to recharge their batteries yourself—again and again.

is almost infinite, the direction and site possibilities of the KITA are increased many times. Fourth, the person administering the kick can manage to be above it all and let the system accomplish the dirty work. Fifth, those who practice it receive some ego satisfaction (one-upmanship), whereas they would find drawing blood abhorrent. Finally, if the employee does complain, he or she can always be accused of being paranoid; there is no tangible evidence of an actual attack.

Now, what does negative KITA accomplish? If I kick you in the rear (physically or psychologically), who is motivated? *I* am motivated; *you* move! Negative KITA does not lead to motivation, but to movement. So:

Idea in Practice

How do you help employees charge themselves up? **Enrich their jobs** by applying these principles:

- Increase individuals' accountability for their work by removing some controls.

- Give people responsibility for a *complete* process or unit of work.

- Make information available directly to employees rather than sending it through their managers first.

- Enable people to take on new, more difficult tasks they haven't handled before.

- Assign individuals specialized tasks that allow them to become experts.

The payoff? Employees gain an enhanced sense of responsibility and achievement, along with new opportunities to learn and grow—continually.

Example: A large firm began enriching stockholder correspondents' jobs by appointing subject-matter experts within each unit—then encouraging other unit members to consult with them before seeking supervisory help. It also held correspondents personally responsible for their communications' quality and quantity. Supervisors who had proofread and signed *all* letters now checked only 10% of them. And rather than harping on production quotas, supervisors no longer discussed daily quantities.

These deceptively modest changes paid big dividends: Within six months, the correspondents' motivation soared—as measured by their answers to questions such as "How many opportunities do you feel you have in your job for making worthwhile contributions?" Equally valuable, their performance noticeably improved, as measured by their communications' quality and accuracy, and their speed of response to stockholders.

Job enrichment isn't easy. Managers may initially fear that they'll no longer be needed once their direct reports take on more responsibility. Employees will likely require time to master new tasks and challenges.

But managers will eventually rediscover their real functions, for example, *developing* staff rather than simply checking their work. And employees' enthusiasm and commitment will ultimately rise—along with your company's overall performance.

Positive KITA

Let us consider motivation. If I say to you, "Do this for me or the company, and in return I will give you a reward, an incentive, more status, a promotion, all the quid pro quos that exist in the industrial organization," am I motivating you? The overwhelming opinion I receive from management people is, "Yes, this is motivation."

I have a year-old schnauzer. When it was a small puppy and I wanted it to move, I kicked it in the rear and it moved. Now that I have finished its obedience training, I hold up a dog biscuit when I want the schnauzer to move. In this instance, who is motivated—I or the dog? The dog wants the biscuit, but it is I who want it to move. Again, I am the one who is motivated, and the dog is the one who moves. In this instance all I did was apply KITA frontally; I exerted a pull instead of a push. When industry wishes to use such positive KITAs, it has available an incredible number and variety of dog biscuits (jelly beans for humans) to wave in front of employees to get them to jump.

Myths About Motivation

Why is KITA not motivation? If I kick my dog (from the front or the back), he will move. And when I want him to move again, what must I do? I must kick him again. Similarly, I can charge a person's battery, and then recharge it, and recharge it again. But it is only when one has a generator of one's own that we can talk about motivation. One then needs no outside stimulation. One *wants* to do it.

With this in mind, we can review some positive KITA personnel practices that were developed as attempts to instill "motivation":

1. Reducing time spent at work

This represents a marvelous way of motivating people to work—getting them off the job! We have reduced (formally and informally) the time spent on the job over the last 50 or 60 years until we are finally on the way to the "6-day weekend." An interesting variant of this approach is the development of off-hour recreation programs. The philosophy here seems to be that those who play together, work together. The fact is that motivated people seek more hours of work, not fewer.

2. Spiraling wages

Have these motivated people? Yes, to seek the next wage increase. Some medievalists still can be heard to say that a good depression will get employees moving. They feel that if rising wages don't or won't do the job, reducing them will.

3. Fringe benefits

Industry has outdone the most welfare-minded of welfare states in dispensing cradle-to-the-grave succor. One company I know of had an informal "fringe benefit of the month club" going for a while. The cost of fringe benefits in this country has reached approximately 25% of the wage dollar, and we still cry for motivation.

People spend less time working for more money and more security than ever before, and the trend cannot be reversed. These benefits are no longer rewards; they are rights. A 6-day week is inhuman, a 10-hour day is exploitation, extended medical coverage is a basic decency, and stock options are the salvation of American initiative. Unless the ante is continuously raised, the psychological reaction of employees is that the company is turning back the clock.

When industry began to realize that both the economic nerve and the lazy nerve of their employees had insatiable appetites, it started to listen to the behavioral scientists who, more out of a humanist tradition than from scientific study, criticized management for not knowing how to deal with people. The next KITA easily followed.

4. Human relations training

More than 30 years of teaching and, in many instances, of practicing psychological approaches to handling people have resulted in costly human relations programs and, in the end, the same question: How do you motivate workers? Here, too, escalations have taken place. Thirty years ago it was necessary to request, "Please don't spit on the floor." Today the same admonition requires three "pleases" before the employee feels that a superior has demonstrated the psychologically proper attitude.

The failure of human relations training to produce motivation led to the conclusion that supervisors or managers themselves were not psychologically true to themselves in their practice of interpersonal decency. So an advanced form of human relations KITA, sensitivity training, was unfolded.

5. Sensitivity training

Do you really, really understand yourself? Do you really, really, really trust other people? Do you really, really, really, really cooperate? The failure of sensitivity training is now being explained, by those who have become opportunistic exploiters of the technique, as a failure to really (five times) conduct proper sensitivity training courses.

With the realization that there are only temporary gains from comfort and economic and interpersonal KITA, personnel managers concluded that the fault lay not in what they were doing, but in the employee's failure to appreciate what they were doing. This opened up the field of communications, a new area of "scientifically" sanctioned KITA.

6. Communications

The professor of communications was invited to join the faculty of management training programs and help in making employees understand what management was doing for them. House organs, briefing sessions, supervisory instruction on the importance of communication, and all sorts of propaganda have proliferated until today there is even an International Council of Industrial Editors. But no motivation resulted, and the obvious thought occurred that perhaps management was not hearing what the employees were saying. That led to the next KITA.

7. Two-way communication

Management ordered morale surveys, suggestion plans, and group participation programs. Then both management and employees were communicating and listening to each other more than ever, but without much improvement in motivation.

The behavioral scientists began to take another look at their conceptions and their data, and they took human relations one step further. A glimmer of truth was beginning to show through in the writings of the so-called higher-order-need psychologists. People, so they said, want to actualize themselves. Unfortunately, the "actualizing" psychologists got mixed up with the human relations psychologists, and a new KITA emerged.

8. Job participation

Though it may not have been the theoretical intention, job participation often became a "give them the big picture" approach. For example, if a man is tightening 10,000 nuts a day on an assembly line with a torque wrench, tell him he is building a Chevrolet. Another approach had the goal of giving employees a "feeling" that they are determining, in some measure, what they do on the job. The goal was to provide a *sense* of achievement rather than a substantive achievement in the task. Real achievement, of course, requires a task that makes it possible.

But still there was no motivation. This led to the inevitable conclusion that the employees must be sick, and therefore to the next KITA.

9. Employee counseling

The initial use of this form of KITA in a systematic fashion can be credited to the Hawthorne experiment of the Western Electric Company during the early 1930s. At that time, it was found that the employees harbored irrational feelings that were interfering with the rational operation of the factory. Counseling in this instance was a means of letting the employees unburden themselves by talking to someone about their problems. Although the counseling techniques were primitive, the program was large indeed.

The counseling approach suffered as a result of experiences during World War II, when the programs themselves were found to be interfering with the operation of the organizations; the counselors had forgotten their role of benevolent listeners and were attempting to do something about the problems that they heard about. Psychological counseling, however, has managed to survive the negative impact of World War II experiences and today is beginning to flourish with renewed sophistication. But, alas, many of these programs, like all the others, do not seem to have lessened the pressure of demands to find out how to motivate workers.

Since KITA results only in short-term movement, it is safe to predict that the cost of these programs will increase steadily and new varieties will be developed as old positive KITAs reach their satiation points.

Hygiene vs. Motivators

Let me rephrase the perennial question this way: How do you install a generator in an employee? A brief review of my motivation-hygiene theory of job attitudes is required before theoretical and practical suggestions can be offered. The theory was first drawn from an examination of events in the lives of engineers and accountants. At least 16 other investigations, using a wide variety of populations (including some in the Communist countries), have since been completed, making the original research one of the most replicated studies in the field of job attitudes.

The findings of these studies, along with corroboration from many other investigations using different procedures, suggest that the factors involved in producing job satisfaction (and motivation) are separate and distinct from the factors that lead to job dissatisfaction. (See "Factors affecting job attitudes as reported in 12 investigations," which is further explained below.) Since separate factors need to be considered, depending on whether job satisfaction or job dissatisfaction is being examined, it follows that these two feelings are not opposites of each other. The opposite of job satisfaction is not job dissatisfaction but, rather, *no* job satisfaction; and similarly, the opposite of job dissatisfaction is not job satisfaction, but *no* job dissatisfaction.

Factors affecting job attitudes as reported in 12 investigations

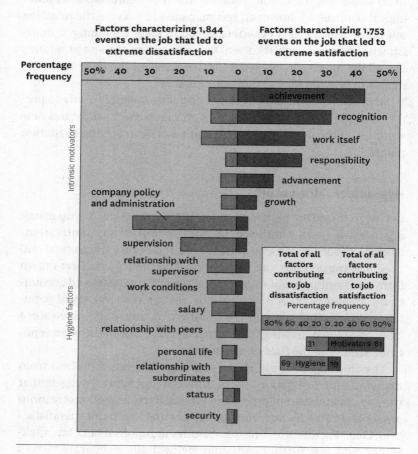

Stating the concept presents a problem in semantics, for we normally think of satisfaction and dissatisfaction as opposites; i.e., what is not satisfying must be dissatisfying, and vice versa. But when it comes to understanding the behavior of people in their jobs, more than a play on words is involved.

Two different needs of human beings are involved here. One set of needs can be thought of as stemming from humankind's animal nature—the built-in drive to avoid pain from the environment, plus all the learned drives that become conditioned to the basic biological needs. For example, hunger, a basic biological drive, makes it necessary to earn money, and then money becomes a specific drive. The other set of needs relates to that unique human characteristic, the ability to achieve and, through achievement, to experience psychological growth. The stimuli for the growth needs are tasks that induce growth; in the industrial setting, they are the job content. Contrariwise, the stimuli inducing pain-avoidance behavior are found in the job environment.

The growth or *motivator* factors that are intrinsic to the job are: achievement, recognition for achievement, the work itself, responsibility, and growth or advancement. The dissatisfaction-avoidance or hygiene (KITA) factors that are extrinsic to the job include: company policy and administration, supervision, interpersonal relationships, working conditions, salary, status, and security.

A composite of the factors that are involved in causing job satisfaction and job dissatisfaction, drawn from samples of 1,685 employees, is shown in "Factors affecting job attitudes as reported in 12 investigations." The results indicate that motivators were the primary cause of satisfaction, and hygiene factors the primary cause of unhappiness on the job. The employees, studied in 12 different investigations, included lower level supervisors, professional women, agricultural administrators, men about to retire from management positions, hospital maintenance personnel, manufacturing supervisors, nurses, food handlers, military officers, engineers, scientists, housekeepers, teachers, technicians, female assemblers, accountants, Finnish foremen, and Hungarian engineers.

They were asked what job events had occurred in their work that had led to extreme satisfaction or extreme dissatisfaction on their part. Their responses are broken down in the figure into percentages of total "positive" job events and of total "negative" job events. (The figures total more than 100% on both the "hygiene" and "motivators" sides because often at least two factors can be attributed to a single event; advancement, for instance, often accompanies assumption of responsibility.)

To illustrate, a typical response involving achievement that had a negative effect for the employee was, "I was unhappy because I didn't do the job successfully." A typical response in the small number of positive job events in the company policy and administration grouping was, "I was happy because the company reorganized the section so that I didn't report any longer to the guy I didn't get along with."

As the lower right-hand part of the figure shows, of all the factors contributing to job satisfaction, 81% were motivators. And of all the factors contributing to the employees' dissatisfaction over their work, 69% involved hygiene elements.

Eternal triangle

There are three general philosophies of personnel management. The first is based on organizational theory, the second on industrial engineering, and the third on behavioral science.

Organizational theorists believe that human needs are either so irrational or so varied and adjustable to specific situations that the major function of personnel management is to be as pragmatic as the occasion demands. If jobs are organized in a proper manner, they reason, the result will be the most efficient job structure, and the most favorable job attitudes will follow as a matter of course.

Industrial engineers hold that humankind is mechanistically oriented and economically motivated and that human needs are best met by attuning the individual to the most efficient work process. The goal of personnel management therefore should be to concoct the most appropriate incentive system and to design the specific working conditions in a way that facilitates the most efficient use of the human machine. By structuring jobs in a manner that leads to the most efficient operation, engineers believe that they can obtain the optimal organization of work and the proper work attitudes.

Behavioral scientists focus on group sentiments, attitudes of individual employees, and the organization's social and psychological climate. This persuasion emphasizes one or more of the various hygiene and motivator needs. Its approach to personnel management is generally to emphasize some form of human relations education, in the hope of instilling healthy employee attitudes and an organizational climate that is considered to be felicitous to human values. The belief is that proper attitudes will lead to efficient job and organizational structure.

There is always a lively debate concerning the overall effectiveness of the approaches of organizational theorists and industrial engineers. Manifestly, both have achieved much. But the nagging question for behavioral scientists has been: What is the cost in human problems that eventually cause more expense to the organization—for instance, turnover, absenteeism, errors, violation of safety rules, strikes, restriction of output, higher wages, and greater fringe benefits? On the other hand, behavioral scientists are hard put to document much manifest improvement in personnel management, using their approach.

The motivation-hygiene theory suggests that work be *enriched* to bring about effective utilization of personnel. Such a systematic attempt to motivate employees by manipulating the motivator factors is just beginning. The term *job enrichment* describes this embryonic movement. An older term, job enlargement, should be avoided because it is associated with past failures stemming from a misunderstanding of the problem. Job enrichment provides the opportunity for the employee's psychological growth, while job enlargement merely makes a job structurally bigger. Since scientific job enrichment is very new, this article only suggests the principles and practical steps that have recently emerged from several successful experiments in industry.

Job loading

In attempting to enrich certain jobs, management often reduces the personal contribution of employees rather than giving them opportunities for growth in their accustomed jobs. Such endeavors, which I shall call horizontal job loading (as opposed to vertical loading, or providing motivator factors), have been the problem of earlier job enlargement programs. Job loading merely enlarges the meaninglessness of the job. Some examples of this approach, and their effect, are:

- Challenging the employee by increasing the amount of production expected. If each tightens 10,000 bolts a day, see if each can tighten 20,000 bolts a day. The arithmetic involved shows that multiplying zero by zero still equals zero.

- Adding another meaningless task to the existing one, usually some routine clerical activity. The arithmetic here is adding zero to zero.

- Rotating the assignments of a number of jobs that need to be enriched. This means washing dishes for a while, then washing silverware. The arithmetic is substituting one zero for another zero.

- Removing the most difficult parts of the assignment in order to free the worker to accomplish more of the less challenging assignments. This traditional industrial engineering approach amounts to subtraction in the hope of accomplishing addition.

These are common forms of horizontal loading that frequently come up in preliminary brainstorming sessions of job enrichment. The principles of vertical loading have not all been worked out as yet, and they remain rather general, but I have furnished seven useful starting points for consideration in "Principles of vertical job loading."

A successful application

An example from a highly successful job enrichment experiment can illustrate the distinction between horizontal and vertical loading of a job. The subjects of this study were the stockholder correspondents employed by a very large corporation. Seemingly, the task required of these carefully selected and highly trained correspondents was quite complex and challenging. But almost all indexes of performance and job attitudes were low, and exit interviewing confirmed that the challenge of the job existed merely as words.

Principles of vertical job loading

Principle	Motivators involved
A. Removing some controls while retaining accountability	Responsibility and personal achievement
B. Increasing the accountability of individuals for own work	Responsibility and recognition
C. Giving a person a complete natural unit of work (module, division, area, and so on)	Responsibility, achievement, and recognition
D. Granting additional authority to employees in their activity; job freedom	Responsibility, achievement, and recognition
E. Making periodic reports directly available to the workers themselves rather than to supervisors	Internal recognition
F. Introducing new and more difficult tasks not previously handled	Growth and learning
G. Assigning individuals specific or specialized tasks, enabling them to become experts	Responsibility, growth, and advancement

A job enrichment project was initiated in the form of an experiment with one group, designated as an achieving unit, having its job enriched by the principles described in "Principles of vertical job loading." A control group continued to do its job in the traditional way. (There were also two "uncommitted" groups of correspondents formed to measure the so-called Hawthorne effect—that is, to gauge whether productivity and attitudes toward the job changed artificially merely because employees sensed that the company was paying more attention to them in doing something different or novel. The results for these groups were substantially the same as for the control group, and for the sake of simplicity I do not deal with them in this summary.) No changes in hygiene were introduced for either group other than those that would have been made anyway, such as normal pay increases.

Employee performance in company experiment

Three-month cumulative average

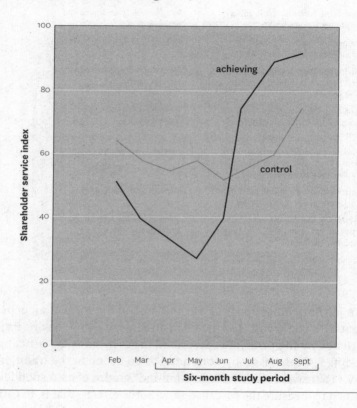

Six-month study period

The changes for the achieving unit were introduced in the first two months, averaging one per week of the seven motivators listed in "Principles of vertical job loading." At the end of six months the members of the achieving unit were found to be outperforming their counterparts in the control group and, in addition, indicated a marked increase in their liking for their jobs. Other results showed that the achieving group had lower absenteeism and, subsequently, a much higher rate of promotion.

"Employee performance in company experiment" illustrates the changes in performance, measured in February and March, before the study period began, and at the end of each month of the study period. The shareholder service index represents quality of letters, including accuracy of information, and speed of response to stockholders' letters of inquiry. The index of a current month was averaged into the average of the two prior months, which means that improvement was harder to obtain if the indexes of the previous months were low. The "achievers" were performing less well before the six-month period started, and their performance service index continued to decline after the introduction of the motivators, evidently because of uncertainty after their newly granted responsibilities. In the third month, however, performance improved, and soon the members of this group had reached a high level of accomplishment.

"Change in attitudes toward tasks in company experiment" shows the two groups' attitudes toward their job, measured at the end of March, just before the first motivator was introduced, and again at the end of September. The correspondents were asked 16 questions, all involving motivation. A typical one was, "As you see it, how many opportunities do you feel that you have in your job for making worthwhile contributions?" The answers were scaled from 1 to 5, with 80 as the maximum possible score. The achievers became much more positive about their job, while the attitude of the control unit remained about the same (the drop is not statistically significant).

How was the job of these correspondents restructured? "Enlargement versus enrichment of correspondents' tasks in company experiment" lists the suggestions made that were deemed to be horizontal loading, and the actual vertical loading changes that were incorporated in the job of the achieving unit. The capital letters under "Principle" after "Vertical Loading" refer to the corresponding letters in "Principles of vertical job loading." The reader will note that the rejected forms of horizontal loading correspond closely to the list of common manifestations I mentioned earlier.

Steps for Job Enrichment

Now that the motivator idea has been described in practice, here are the steps that managers should take in instituting the principle with their employees:

1. Select those jobs in which a) the investment in industrial engineering does not make changes too costly, b) attitudes are poor, c) hygiene is becoming very costly, and d) motivation will make a difference in performance.

2. Approach these jobs with the conviction that they can be changed. Years of tradition have led managers to believe that job content is sacrosanct and the only scope of action that they have is in ways of stimulating people.

3. Brainstorm a list of changes that may enrich the jobs, without concern for their practicality.

4. Screen the list to eliminate suggestions that involve hygiene, rather than actual motivation.

5. Screen the list for generalities, such as "give them more responsibility," that are rarely followed in practice. This might seem obvious, but the motivator words have never left industry; the substance has just been rationalized and organized out. Words like "responsibility," "growth," "achievement," and "challenge," for example, have been elevated to the lyrics of the patriotic anthem for all organizations. It is the old problem typified by the pledge of allegiance to the flag being more important than contributions to the country—of following the form, rather than the substance.

6. Screen the list to eliminate any *horizontal* loading suggestions.

7. Avoid direct participation by the employees whose jobs are to be enriched. Ideas they have expressed previously certainly constitute a valuable source for recommended changes, but their direct involvement contaminates the process with human relations *hygiene* and, more specifically, gives them

Change in attitudes toward tasks in company experiment

Mean scores at beginning and end of six-month period

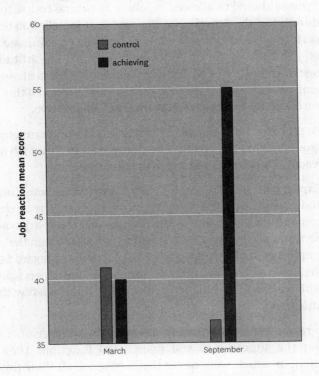

only a *sense* of making a contribution. The job is to be changed, and it is the content that will produce the motivation, not attitudes about being involved or the challenge inherent in setting up a job. That process will be over shortly, and it is what the employees will be doing from then on that will determine their motivation. A sense of participation will result only in short-term movement.

8. In the initial attempts at job enrichment, set up a controlled experiment. At least two equivalent groups should be chosen,

one an experimental unit in which the motivators are systematically introduced over a period of time, and the other one a control group in which no changes are made. For both groups, hygiene should be allowed to follow its natural course for the duration of the experiment. Pre- and post-installation tests of performance and job attitudes are necessary to evaluate the effectiveness of the job enrichment program. The attitude test must be limited to motivator items in order to divorce employees' views of the jobs they are given from all the surrounding hygiene feelings that they might have.

9. Be prepared for a drop in performance in the experimental group the first few weeks. The changeover to a new job may lead to a temporary reduction in efficiency.

10. Expect your first-line supervisors to experience some anxiety and hostility over the changes you are making. The anxiety comes from their fear that the changes will result in poorer performance for their unit. Hostility will arise when the employees start assuming what the supervisors regard as their own responsibility for performance. The supervisor without checking duties to perform may then be left with little to do.

After successful experiment, however, the supervisors usually discover the supervisory and managerial functions they have neglected, or which were never theirs because all their time was given over to checking the work of their subordinates. For example, in the R&D division of one large chemical company I know of, the supervisors of the laboratory assistants were theoretically responsible for their training and evaluation. These functions, however, had come to be performed in a routine, unsubstantial fashion. After the job enrichment program, during which the supervisors were not merely passive observers of the assistants' performance, the supervisors actually were devoting their time to reviewing performance and administering thorough training.

Enlargement versus enrichment of correspondents' tasks in company experiment

Horizontal loading suggestions rejected

Firm quotas could be set for letters to be answered each day, using a rate that would be hard to reach.

The secretaries could type the letters themselves, as well as compose them, or take on any other clerical functions.

All difficult or complex inquiries could be channeled to a few secretaries so that the remainder could achieve high rates of output. These jobs could be exchanged from time to time.

The secretaries could be rotated through units handling different customers and then sent back to their own units.

Vertical loading suggestions adopted	Principle
Subject matter experts were appointed within each unit for other members of the unit to consult before seeking supervisory help. (The supervisor had been answering all specialized and difficult questions.)	G
Correspondents signed their own names on letters. (The supervisor had been signing all letters.)	B
The work of the more experienced correspondents was proofread less frequently by supervisors and was done at the correspondents' desks, dropping verification from 100% to 10%. (Previously, all correspondents' letters had been checked by the supervisor.)	A
Production was discussed, but only in terms such as "a full day's work is expected." As time went on, this was no longer mentioned. (Before, the group had been constantly reminded of the number of letters that needed to be answered.)	D
Outgoing mail went directly to the mailroom without going over supervisor's desks. (The letters had always been routed through the supervisors.)	A
Correspondents were encouraged to answer letters in a more personalized way. (Reliance on the form-letter approach had been standard practice.)	C
Each correspondent was held personally responsible for the quality and accuracy of letters. (This responsibility had been the province of the supervisor and the verifier.)	B, E

What has been called an employee-centered style of supervision will come about not through education of supervisors, but by changing the jobs that they do.

———————

Job enrichment will not be a one-time proposition, but a continuous management function. The initial changes should last for a very long period of time. There are a number of reasons for this:

- The changes should bring the job up to the level of challenge commensurate with the skill that was hired.

- Those who have still more ability eventually will be able to demonstrate it better and win promotion to higher level jobs.

- The very nature of motivators, as opposed to hygiene factors, is that they have a much longer-term effect on employees' attitudes. It is possible that the job will have to be enriched again, but this will not occur as frequently as the need for hygiene.

Not all jobs can be enriched, nor do all jobs need to be enriched. If only a small percentage of the time and money that is now devoted to hygiene, however, were given to job enrichment efforts, the return in human satisfaction and economic gain would be one of the largest dividends that industry and society have ever reaped through their efforts at better personnel management.

The argument for job enrichment can be summed up quite simply: If you have employees on a job, use them. If you can't use them on the job, get rid of them, either via automation or by selecting someone with lesser ability. If you can't use them and you can't get rid of them, you will have a motivation problem.

Originally published in September 1987. Reprint R0301F.

The Set-Up-to-Fail Syndrome

by Jean-François Manzoni and Jean-Louis Barsoux

WHEN AN EMPLOYEE FAILS—or even just performs poorly—managers typically do not blame themselves. The employee doesn't understand the work, a manager might contend. Or the employee isn't driven to succeed, can't set priorities, or won't take direction. Whatever the reason, the problem is assumed to be the employee's fault—and the employee's responsibility.

But is it? Sometimes, of course, the answer is yes. Some employees are not up to their assigned tasks and never will be, for lack of knowledge, skill, or simple desire. But sometimes—and we would venture to say often—an employee's poor performance can be blamed largely on his boss.

Perhaps "blamed" is too strong a word, but it is directionally correct. In fact, our research strongly suggests that bosses—albeit accidentally and usually with the best intentions—are often complicit in an employee's lack of success. (See the sidebar "About the Research.") How? By creating and reinforcing a dynamic that essentially sets up perceived underperformers to fail. If the Pygmalion effect describes the dynamic in which an individual lives up to great expectations, the set-up-to-fail syndrome explains the opposite. It describes a dynamic in which employees perceived to be mediocre or weak performers live down to the low expectations their managers have for them. The result is that they often end up leaving the organization—either of their own volition or not.

The syndrome usually begins surreptitiously. The initial impetus can be performance related, such as when an employee loses a client, undershoots a target, or misses a deadline. Often, however, the trigger is less specific. An employee is transferred into a division with a lukewarm recommendation from a previous boss. Or perhaps the boss and the employee don't really get along on a personal basis—several studies have indeed shown that compatibility between boss and subordinate, based on similarity of attitudes, values, or social characteristics, can have a significant impact on a boss's impressions. In any case, the syndrome is set in motion when the boss begins to worry that the employee's performance is not up to par.

The boss then takes what seems like the obvious action in light of the subordinate's perceived shortcomings: he increases the time and attention he focuses on the employee. He requires the employee to get approval before making decisions, asks to see more paperwork documenting those decisions, or watches the employee at meetings more closely and critiques his comments more intensely.

These actions are intended to boost performance and prevent the subordinate from making errors. Unfortunately, however, subordinates often interpret the heightened supervision as a lack of trust and confidence. In time, because of low expectations, they come to doubt their own thinking and ability, and they lose the motivation to make autonomous decisions or to take any action at all. The boss, they figure, will just question everything they do—or do it himself anyway.

Ironically, the boss sees the subordinate's withdrawal as proof that the subordinate is indeed a poor performer. The subordinate, after all, isn't contributing his ideas or energy to the organization. So what does the boss do? He increases his pressure and supervision again—watching, questioning, and double-checking everything the subordinate does. Eventually, the subordinate gives up on his dreams of making a meaningful contribution. Boss and subordinate typically settle into a routine that is not really satisfactory but, aside from periodic clashes, is otherwise bearable for them. In the

Idea in Brief

That darned employee! His performance keeps deteriorating—*despite* your close monitoring. What's going on?

Brace yourself: *You* may be at fault, by unknowingly triggering the **set-up-to-fail syndrome**. Employees whom you (perhaps falsely) view as weak performers live *down* to your expectations. Here's how:

1. You start with a positive relationship.

2. Something—a missed deadline, a lost client—makes you question the employee's performance. You begin micromanaging him.

3. Suspecting your reduced confidence, the employee starts doubting *himself*. He stops giving his best, responds mechanically to your controls, and avoids decisions.

4. You view his new behavior as additional proof of mediocrity—and tighten the screws further.

Why not just fire him? Because you're likely to repeat the pattern with others. Better to *reverse* the dynamic instead. Unwinding the set-up-to-fail spiral actually pays big dividends: Your company gets the best from your employees— and from you.

worst-case scenario, the boss's intense intervention and scrutiny end up paralyzing the employee into inaction and consume so much of the boss's time that the employee quits or is fired. (See "The set-up-to-fail syndrome: No harm intended: A relationship spirals from bad to worse.")

Perhaps the most daunting aspect of the set-up-to-fail syndrome is that it is self-fulfilling and self-reinforcing—it is the quintessential vicious circle. The process is self-fulfilling because the boss's actions contribute to the very behavior that is expected from weak performers. It is self-reinforcing because the boss's low expectations, in being fulfilled by his subordinates, trigger more of the same behavior on his part, which in turn triggers more of the same behavior on the part of subordinates. And on and on, unintentionally, the relationship spirals downward.

A case in point is the story of Steve, a manufacturing supervisor for a *Fortune* 100 company. When we first met Steve, he came across

Idea in Practice

How Set-Up-to-Fail Starts

A manager categorizes employees as "in" or "out," based on:

- early *perceptions* of employees' motivation, initiative, creativity, strategic perspectives;
- previous bosses' impressions;
- an early mishap; and
- boss-subordinate incompatibility.

The manager then notices *only* evidence supporting his categorization, while dismissing contradictory evidence. The boss also treats the groups differently:

- "In" groups get autonomy, feedback, and expressions of confidence.
- "Out" groups get controlling, formal management emphasizing rules.

The Costs of Set-Up-to-Fail

This syndrome hurts everyone:

- *Employees* stop volunteering ideas and information and asking for help, avoid contact with bosses, or grow defensive.
- The *organization* fails to get the most from employees.
- The *boss* loses energy to attend to other activities. His reputation suffers as other employees deem him unfair.
- *Team spirit* wilts as targeted performers are alienated and strong performers are overburdened.

How to Reverse Set-Up-to-Fail

If the syndrome hasn't started, prevent it:

- Establish expectations with new employees early. Loosen

as highly motivated, energetic, and enterprising. He was on top of his operation, monitoring problems and addressing them quickly. His boss expressed great confidence in him and gave him an excellent performance rating. Because of his high performance, Steve was chosen to lead a new production line considered essential to the plant's future.

In his new job, Steve reported to Jeff, who had just been promoted to a senior management position at the plant. In the first few weeks of the relationship, Jeff periodically asked Steve to write up short analyses of significant quality-control rejections. Although Jeff didn't really explain this to Steve at the time, his request had the reins as they master their jobs.

- Regularly challenge your own assumptions. Ask: "What are the *facts* regarding this employee's performance?" "Is he really that bad?"

- Convey openness, letting employees challenge your opinions. They'll feel comfortable discussing their performance and relationship with you.

If the syndrome has already erupted, discuss the dynamic with the employee:

1. Choose a neutral, nonthreatening location; use affirming language ("Let's discuss our relationship and roles"); and acknowledge your part in the tension.

2. Agree on the employee's weaknesses and strengths. Support assessments with facts, not feelings.

3. Unearth causes of the weaknesses. Do you disagree on priorities? Does your employee lack specific knowledge or skills? Ask: "How is my behavior making things worse for you?"

4. Identify ways to boost performance. Training? New experiences? Decide the quantity and type of supervision you'll provide. Affirm your desire to improve matters.

5. Agree to communicate more openly: "Next time I do something that communicates low expectations, can you let me know immediately?"

two major objectives: to generate information that would help both of them learn the new production process, and to help Steve develop the habit of systematically performing root cause analysis of quality-related problems. Also, being new on the job himself, Jeff wanted to show his own boss that he was on top of the operation.

Unaware of Jeff's motives, Steve balked. Why, he wondered, should he submit reports on information he understood and monitored himself? Partly due to lack of time, partly in response to what he considered interference from his boss, Steve invested little energy in the reports. Their tardiness and below-average quality annoyed Jeff, who began to suspect that Steve was not a particularly proactive manager. When he asked for the reports again, he was more forceful. For Steve, this merely confirmed that Jeff did not trust him. He withdrew more and more from interaction with him, meeting his demands with increased passive resistance. Before long, Jeff became convinced that Steve was not effective enough and couldn't handle his job without help. He started to supervise Steve's every move—to Steve's predictable dismay. One year after excitedly taking on the new production line, Steve was so dispirited he was thinking of quitting.

How can managers break the set-up-to-fail syndrome? Before answering that question, let's take a closer look at the dynamics that set the syndrome in motion and keep it going.

Deconstructing the Syndrome

We said earlier that the set-up-to-fail syndrome usually starts surreptitiously—that is, it is a dynamic that usually creeps up on the boss and the subordinate until suddenly both of them realize that the relationship has gone sour. But underlying the syndrome are several assumptions about weaker performers that bosses appear to accept uniformly. Our research shows, in fact, that executives typically compare weaker performers with stronger performers using the following descriptors:

- less motivated, less energetic, and less likely to go beyond the call of duty;

- more passive when it comes to taking charge of problems or projects;

- less aggressive about anticipating problems;

- less innovative and less likely to suggest ideas;

- more parochial in their vision and strategic perspective;

- more prone to hoard information and assert their authority, making them poor bosses to their own subordinates.

It is not surprising that on the basis of these assumptions, bosses tend to treat weaker and stronger performers very differently. Indeed, numerous studies have shown that up to 90% of all managers treat some subordinates as though they were members of an in-group, while they consign others to membership in an out-group. Members of the in-group are considered the trusted collaborators and therefore receive more autonomy, feedback, and expressions of confidence from their bosses. The boss-subordinate relationship for this group is one of mutual trust and reciprocal influence. Members of the out-group, on the other hand, are regarded more as hired hands and are managed in a more formal, less personal way, with more emphasis on rules, policies, and authority. (For more on how bosses treat weaker and stronger performers differently, see the chart "In with the In Crowd, Out with the Out.")

Why do managers categorize subordinates into either in-groups or out-groups? For the same reason that we tend to typecast our family, friends, and acquaintances: it makes life easier. Labeling is something we all do, because it allows us to function more efficiently. It saves time by providing rough-and-ready guides for interpreting events and interacting with others. Managers, for instance, use categorical thinking to figure out quickly who should get what tasks. That's the good news.

The downside of categorical thinking is that in organizations it leads to premature closure. Having made up his mind about a subordinate's limited ability and poor motivation, a manager is likely to notice supporting evidence while selectively dismissing contrary evidence. (For example, a manager might interpret a terrific new product idea from an out-group subordinate as a lucky onetime event.) Unfortunately for some subordinates, several studies show that bosses tend to make decisions about in-groups and out-groups even as early as five days into their relationships with employees.

Are bosses aware of this sorting process and of their different approaches to "in" and "out" employees? Definitely. In fact, the bosses we have studied, regardless of nationality, company, or personal background, were usually quite conscious of behaving in a more controlling way with perceived weaker performers. Some of them

About the Research

This article is based on two studies designed to understand better the causal relationship between leadership style and subordinate performance—in other words, to explore how bosses and subordinates mutually influence each other's behavior. The first study, which comprised surveys, interviews, and observations, involved 50 boss-subordinate pairs in four manufacturing operations in *Fortune* 100 companies. The second study, involving an informal survey of about 850 senior managers attending INSEAD executive-development programs over the last three years, was done to test and refine the findings generated by the first study. The executives in the second study represented a wide diversity of nationalities, industries, and personal backgrounds.

---

preferred to label this approach as "supportive and helpful." Many of them also acknowledged that—although they tried not to—they tended to become impatient with weaker performers more easily than with stronger performers. By and large, however, managers are aware of the controlling nature of their behavior toward perceived weaker performers. For them, this behavior is not an error in implementation; it is intentional.

What bosses typically do *not* realize is that their tight controls end up hurting subordinates' performance by undermining their motivation in two ways: first, by depriving subordinates of autonomy on the job and, second, by making them feel undervalued. Tight controls are an indication that the boss assumes the subordinate can't perform well without strict guidelines. When the subordinate senses these low expectations, it can undermine his self-confidence. This is particularly problematic because numerous studies confirm that people perform up or down to the levels their bosses expect from them or, indeed, to the levels they expect from themselves.[1]

Of course, executives often tell us, "Oh, but I'm very careful about this issue of expectations. I exert more control over my underperformers, but I make sure that it does not come across as a lack of trust or confidence in their ability." We believe what these executives tell us. That is, we believe that they do try hard to disguise their intentions. When we talk to their subordinates, however, we find

The Set-Up-to-Fail Syndrome

No harm intended: A relationship spirals from bad to worse

1. Before the set-up-to-fail syndrome begins, the boss and the subordinate are typically engaged in a positive, or at least neutral, relationship.

2. The triggering event in the set-up-to-fail syndrome is often minor or surreptitious. The subordinate may miss a deadline, lose a client, or submit a subpar report. In other cases, the syndrome's genesis is the boss, who distances himself from the subordinate for personal or social reasons unrelated to performance.

3. Reacting to the triggering event, the boss increases his supervision of the subordinate, gives more specific instructions, and wrangles longer over courses of action.

4. The subordinate responds by beginning to suspect a lack of confidence and senses he's not part of the boss's in-group anymore.

   He starts to withdraw emotionally from the boss and from work. He may also fight to change the boss's image of him, reaching too high or running too fast to be effective.

5. The boss interprets this problem-hoarding, overreaching, or tentativeness as signs that the subordinate has poor judgment and weak capabilities. If the subordinate does perform well, the boss does not acknowledge it or considers it a lucky "one off."

   He limits the subordinate's discretion, withholds social contact, and shows, with increasing openness, his lack of confidence in and frustration with the subordinate.

6. The subordinate feels boxed in and underappreciated. He increasingly withdraws from his boss and from work. He may even resort to ignoring instructions, openly disputing the boss, and occasionally lashing out because of feelings of rejection.

   In general, he performs his job mechanically and devotes more energy to self-protection. Moreover, he refers all nonroutine decisions to the boss or avoids contact with him.

7. The boss feels increasingly frustrated and is now convinced that the subordinate cannot perform without intense oversight. He makes this known by his words and deeds, further undermining the subordinate's confidence and prompting inaction.

8. When the set-up-to-fail syndrome is in full swing, the boss pressures and controls the subordinate during interactions. Otherwise, he avoids contact and gives the subordinate routine assignments only.

   For his part, the subordinate shuts down or leaves, either in dismay, frustration, or anger.

that these efforts are for the most part futile. In fact, our research shows that most employees can—and do—"read their boss's mind." In particular, they know full well whether they fit into their boss's in-group or out-group. All they have to do is compare how they are treated with how their more highly regarded colleagues are treated.

Just as the boss's assumptions about weaker performers and the right way to manage them explains his complicity in the set-up-to-fail syndrome, the subordinate's assumptions about what the boss is thinking explain his own complicity. The reason? When people perceive disapproval, criticism, or simply a lack of confidence and appreciation, they tend to shut down—a behavioral phenomenon that manifests itself in several ways.

Primarily, shutting down means disconnecting intellectually and emotionally. Subordinates simply stop giving their best. They grow

---

In with the In Crowd, Out with the Out

Boss's behavior toward perceived stronger performers	Boss's behavior toward perceived weaker performers
Discusses project objectives, with a limited focus on project implementation. Gives subordinate the freedom to choose his own approach to solving problems or reaching goals.	Is directive when discussing tasks and goals. Focuses on what needs get done as well as how it should get done.
Treats unfavorable variances, mistakes, or incorrect judgments as learning opportunities.	Pays close attention to unfavorable variances, mistakes, or incorrect judgments.
Makes himself available, as in "let me know if I can help." Initiates casual and personal conversations.	Makes himself available to subordinate on a need-to-see basis. Bases conversations primarily on work-related topics.
Is open to subordinate's suggestions and discusses them with interest.	Pays little interest to subordinate's comments or suggestions about how and why work is done.
Gives subordinate interesting and challenging stretch assignments. Often allows subordinate to choose his own assignments.	Reluctantly gives subordinate anything but routine assignments. When handing out assignments, gives subordinate little choice. Monitors subordinate heavily.
Solicits opinions from subordinate on organizational strategy, execution, policy, and procedures.	Rarely asks subordinate for input about organizational or work-related matters.
Often defers to subordinate's opinion in disagreements.	Usually imposes own views in disagreements.
Praises subordinate for work well done.	Emphasizes what the subordinate is doing poorly.

---

tired of being overruled, and they lose the will to fight for their ideas. As one subordinate put it, "My boss tells me how to execute every detail. Rather than arguing with him, I've ended up wanting to say, 'Come on, just tell me what you want me to do, and I'll go do it.' You become a robot." Another perceived weak performer explained, "When my boss tells me to do something, I just do it mechanically."

Shutting down also involves disengaging personally—essentially reducing contact with the boss. Partly, this disengagement is motivated by the nature of previous exchanges that have tended to be negative in tone. As one subordinate admitted, "I used to initiate much more contact with my boss until the only thing I received was negative feedback; then I started shying away."

Besides the risk of a negative reaction, perceived weaker performers are concerned with not tainting their images further. Following the often-heard aphorism "Better to keep quiet and look like a fool than to open your mouth and prove it," they avoid asking for help for fear of further exposing their limitations. They also tend to volunteer less information—a simple "heads up" from a perceived underperformer can cause the boss to overreact and jump into action when none is required. As one perceived weak performer recalled, "I just wanted to let my boss know about a small matter, only slightly out of the routine, but as soon as I mentioned it, he was all over my case. I should have kept my mouth closed. I do now."

Finally, shutting down can mean becoming defensive. Many perceived underperformers start devoting more energy to self-justification. Anticipating that they will be personally blamed for failures, they seek to find excuses early. They end up spending a lot of time looking in the rearview mirror and less time looking at the road ahead. In some cases—as in the case of Steve, the manufacturing supervisor described earlier—this defensiveness can lead to noncompliance or even systematic opposition to the boss's views. While this idea of a weak subordinate going head to head with his boss may seem irrational, it may reflect what Albert Camus once observed: "When deprived of choice, the only freedom left is the freedom to say no."

The Syndrome Is Costly

There are two obvious costs of the set-up-to-fail syndrome: the emotional cost paid by the subordinate and the organizational cost associated with the company's failure to get the best out of an employee. Yet there are other costs to consider, some of them indirect and long term.

The boss pays for the syndrome in several ways. First, uneasy relationships with perceived low performers often sap the boss's emotional and physical energy. It can be quite a strain to keep up a facade of courtesy and pretend everything is fine when both parties know it is not. In addition, the energy devoted to trying to fix these relationships or improve the subordinate's performance through increased supervision prevents the boss from attending to other activities—which often frustrates or even angers the boss.

Furthermore, the syndrome can take its toll on the boss's reputation, as other employees in the organization observe his behavior toward weaker performers. If the boss's treatment of a subordinate is deemed unfair or unsupportive, observers will be quick to draw their lessons. One outstanding performer commented on his boss's controlling and hypercritical behavior toward another subordinate: "It made us all feel like we're expendable." As organizations increasingly espouse the virtues of learning and empowerment, managers must cultivate their reputations as coaches, as well as get results.

The set-up-to-fail syndrome also has serious consequences for any team. A lack of faith in perceived weaker performers can tempt bosses to overload those whom they consider superior performers; bosses want to entrust critical assignments to those who can be counted on to deliver reliably and quickly and to those who will go beyond the call of duty because of their strong sense of shared fate. As one boss half-jokingly said, "Rule number one: if you want something done, give it to someone who's busy—there's a reason why that person is busy."

An increased workload may help perceived superior performers learn to manage their time better, especially as they start to delegate to their own subordinates more effectively. In many cases, however, these performers simply absorb the greater load and higher stress which, over time, takes a personal toll and decreases the attention they can devote to other dimensions of their jobs, particularly those yielding longer-term benefits. In the worst-case scenario, overburdening strong performers can lead to burnout.

Team spirit can also suffer from the progressive alienation of one or more perceived low performers. Great teams share a sense of enthusiasm and commitment to a common mission. Even when members of the boss's out-group try to keep their pain to themselves, other team members feel the strain. One manager recalled the discomfort experienced by the whole team as they watched their boss grill one of their peers every week. As he explained, "A team is like a functioning organism. If one member is suffering, the whole team feels that pain."

In addition, alienated subordinates often do not keep their suffering to themselves. In the corridors or over lunch, they seek out sympathetic ears to vent their recriminations and complaints, not only wasting their own time but also pulling their colleagues away from productive work. Instead of focusing on the team's mission, valuable time and energy is diverted to the discussion of internal politics and dynamics.

Finally, the set-up-to-fail syndrome has consequences for the subordinates of the perceived weak performers. Consider the weakest kid in the school yard who gets pummeled by a bully. The abused child often goes home and pummels his smaller, weaker siblings. So it is with the people who are in the boss's out-group. When they have to manage their own employees, they frequently replicate the behavior that their bosses show to them. They fail to recognize good results or, more often, supervise their employees excessively.

Breaking Out Is Hard to Do

The set-up-to-fail syndrome is not irreversible. Subordinates can break out of it, but we have found that to be rare. The subordinate must consistently deliver such superior results that the boss is forced to change the employee from out-group to in-group status—a phenomenon made difficult by the context in which these subordinates operate. It is hard for subordinates to impress their bosses when they must work on unchallenging tasks, with no autonomy and limited resources; it is also hard for them to persist and maintain high standards when they receive little encouragement from their bosses.

Furthermore, even if the subordinate achieves better results, it may take some time for them to register with the boss because of his selective observation and recall. Indeed, research shows that bosses tend to attribute the good things that happen to weaker performers to external factors rather than to their efforts and ability (while the opposite is true for perceived high performers: successes tend to be seen as theirs, and failures tend to be attributed to external uncontrollable factors). The subordinate will therefore need to achieve a string of successes in order to have the boss even contemplate revising the initial categorization. Clearly, it takes a special kind of courage, self-confidence, competence, and persistence on the part of the subordinate to break out of the syndrome.

Instead, what often happens is that members of the out-group set excessively ambitious goals for themselves to impress the boss quickly and powerfully—promising to hit a deadline three weeks early, for instance, or attacking six projects at the same time, or simply attempting to handle a large problem without help. Sadly, such superhuman efforts are usually just that. And in setting goals so high that they are bound to fail, the subordinates also come across as having had very poor judgment in the first place.

The set-up-to-fail syndrome is not restricted to incompetent bosses. We have seen it happen to people perceived within their organizations to be excellent bosses. Their mismanagement of some subordinates need not prevent them from achieving success, particularly when they and the perceived superior performers achieve high levels of individual performance. However, those bosses could be even more successful to the team, the organization, and themselves if they could break the syndrome.

Getting It Right

As a general rule, the first step in solving a problem is recognizing that one exists. This observation is especially relevant to the set-up-to-fail syndrome because of its self-fulfilling and self-reinforcing nature. Interrupting the syndrome requires that a manager understand the dynamic and, particularly, that he accept the possibility that his own behavior may be contributing to a subordinate's underperformance. The next step toward cracking the syndrome, however, is more difficult: it requires a carefully planned and structured intervention that takes the form of one (or several) candid conversations meant to bring to the surface and untangle the unhealthy dynamics that define the boss and the subordinate's relationship. The goal of such an intervention is to bring about a sustainable increase in the subordinate's performance while progressively reducing the boss's involvement.

It would be difficult—and indeed, detrimental—to provide a detailed script of what this kind of conversation should sound like. A boss who rigidly plans for this conversation with a subordinate will not be able to engage in real dialogue with him, because real dialogue requires flexibility. As a guiding framework, however, we offer five components that characterize effective interventions. Although they are not strictly sequential steps, all five components should be part of these interventions.

First, the boss must create the right context for the discussion

He must, for instance, select a time and place to conduct the meeting so that it presents as little threat as possible to the subordinate. A neutral location may be more conducive to open dialogue than an office where previous and perhaps unpleasant conversations have taken place. The boss must also use affirming language when asking the subordinate to meet with him. The session should not be billed as "feedback," because such terms may suggest baggage from the past. "Feedback" could also be taken to mean that the conversation will be one-directional, a monologue delivered by the boss to the subordinate. Instead, the intervention should be described as a meeting to discuss the performance of the subordinate, the role of the boss, and the relationship between the subordinate and the boss. The boss might even acknowledge that he feels tension in the relationship and wants to use the conversation as a way to decrease it.

Finally, in setting the context, the boss should tell the perceived weaker performer that he would genuinely like the interaction to be an open dialogue. In particular, he should acknowledge that he may be partially responsible for the situation and that his own behavior toward the subordinate is fair game for discussion.

Second, the boss and the subordinate must use the intervention process to come to an agreement on the symptoms of the problem

Few employees are ineffective in all aspects of their performance. And few—if any—employees desire to do poorly on the job. Therefore, it is critical that the intervention result in a mutual understanding of the specific job responsibilities in which the subordinate is weak. In the case of Steve and Jeff, for instance, an exhaustive sorting of the evidence might have led to an agreement that Steve's underperformance was not universal but instead largely confined to the quality of the reports he submitted (or failed to submit). In another situation, it might be agreed that a purchasing manager was weak when it came to finding off-shore suppliers and to voicing his ideas in meetings. Or a new investment professional and his boss might come to agree that his performance was subpar when it came to timing the sales and purchase of stocks, but they might also agree that his financial analysis of stocks was quite strong. The idea here is that before working to improve performance or reduce tension in a relationship, an agreement must be reached about what areas of performance contribute to the contentiousness.

We used the word "evidence" above in discussing the case of Steve and Jeff. That is because a boss needs to back up his performance assessments with facts and data—that is, if the intervention is to be useful. They cannot be based on feelings—as in Jeff telling

Steve, "I just have the feeling you're not putting enough energy into the reports." Instead, Jeff needs to describe what a good report should look like and the ways in which Steve's reports fall short. Likewise, the subordinate must be allowed—indeed, encouraged—to defend his performance, compare it with colleagues' work, and point out areas in which he is strong. After all, just because it is the boss's opinion does not make it a fact.

Third, the boss and the subordinate should arrive at a common understanding of what might be causing the weak performance in certain areas

Once the areas of weak performance have been identified, it is time to unearth the reasons for those weaknesses. Does the subordinate have limited skills in organizing work, managing his time, or working with others? Is he lacking knowledge or capabilities? Do the boss and the subordinate agree on their priorities? Maybe the subordinate has been paying less attention to a particular dimension of his work because he does not realize its importance to the boss. Does the subordinate become less effective under pressure? Does he have lower standards for performance than the boss does?

It is also critical in the intervention that the boss bring up the subject of his own behavior toward the subordinate and how this affects the subordinate's performance. The boss might even try to describe the dynamics of the set-up-to-fail syndrome. "Does my behavior toward you make things worse for you?" he might ask, or, "What am I doing that is leading you to feel that I am putting too much pressure on you?"

This component of the discussion also needs to make explicit the assumptions that the boss and the subordinate have thus far been making about each other's intentions. Many misunderstandings start with untested assumptions. For example, Jeff might have said, "When you did not supply me with the reports I asked for, I came to the conclusion that you were not very proactive." That would have allowed Steve to bring his buried assumptions into the open. "No," he might have answered, "I just reacted negatively because you asked for the reports in writing, which I took as a sign of excessive control."

Fourth, the boss and the subordinate should arrive at an agreement about their performance objectives and on their desire to have the relationship move forward

In medicine, a course of treatment follows the diagnosis of an illness. Things are a bit more complex when repairing organizational dysfunction, since modifying behavior and developing complex skills can be more difficult than taking a few pills. Still, the principle that applies to medicine also applies to business: boss and subordinate must use the intervention to plot a course of treatment regarding the root problems they have jointly identified.

The contract between boss and subordinate should identify the ways they can improve on their skills, knowledge, experience, or personal relationship. It should also include an explicit discussion of how much and what type of future supervision the boss will have. No boss, of course, should suddenly abdicate his involvement; it is legitimate for bosses to monitor subordinates' work, particularly when a subordinate has shown limited abilities in one or more facets of his job. From the subordinate's point of view, however, such involvement by the boss is more likely to be accepted, and possibly even welcomed, if the goal is to help the subordinate develop and improve over time. Most subordinates can accept temporary involvement that is meant to decrease as their performance improves. The problem is intense monitoring that never seems to go away.

Fifth, the boss and the subordinate should agree to communicate more openly in the future

The boss could say, "Next time I do something that communicates low expectations, can you let me know immediately?" And the subordinate might say, or be encouraged to say, "Next time I do something that aggravates you or that you do not understand, can you also let me know right away?" Those simple requests can open the door to a more honest relationship almost instantly.

No Easy Answer

Our research suggests that interventions of this type do not take place very often. Face-to-face discussions about a subordinate's performance tend to come high on the list of workplace situations people would rather avoid, because such conversations have the potential to make both parties feel threatened or embarrassed. Subordinates are reluctant to trigger the discussion because they are worried about coming across as thin-skinned or whiny. Bosses tend to avoid initiating these talks because they are concerned about the way the subordinate might react; the discussion could force the boss to make explicit his lack of confidence in the subordinate, in turn putting the subordinate on the defensive and making the situation worse.[2]

As a result, bosses who observe the dynamics of the set-up-to-fail syndrome being played out may be tempted to avoid an explicit discussion. Instead, they will proceed tacitly by trying to encourage their perceived weak performers. That approach has the short-term benefit of bypassing the discomfort of an open discussion, but it has three major disadvantages.

First, a one-sided approach on the part of the boss is less likely to lead to lasting improvement because it focuses on only one symptom of the problem—the boss's behavior. It does not address the subordinate's role in the underperformance.

Second, even if the boss's encouragement were successful in improving the employee's performance, a unilateral approach would limit what both he and the subordinate could otherwise learn from a more up-front handling of the problem. The subordinate, in particular, would not have the benefit of observing and learning from how his boss handled the difficulties in their relationship—problems the subordinate may come across someday with the people he manages.

Finally, bosses trying to modify their behavior in a unilateral way often end up going overboard; they suddenly give the subordinate more autonomy and responsibility than he can handle productively. Predictably, the subordinate fails to deliver to the boss's satisfaction, which leaves the boss even more frustrated and convinced that the subordinate cannot function without intense supervision.

We are not saying that intervention is always the best course of action. Sometimes, intervention is not possible or desirable. There may be, for instance, overwhelming evidence that the subordinate is not capable of doing his job. He was a hiring or promotion mistake, which is best handled by removing him from the position. In other cases, the relationship between the boss and the subordinate is too far gone—too much damage has occurred to repair it. And finally, sometimes bosses are too busy and under too much pressure to invest the kind of resources that intervention involves.

Yet often the biggest obstacle to effective intervention is the boss's mind-set. When a boss believes that a subordinate is a weak performer and, on top of everything else, that person also aggravates him, he is not going to be able to cover up his feelings with words; his underlying convictions will come out in the meeting. That is why preparation for the intervention is crucial. Before even deciding to have a meeting, the boss must separate emotion from reality. Was the situation always as bad as it is now? Is the subordinate really as bad as I think he is? What is the hard evidence I have for that belief? Could there be other factors, aside from performance, that have led me to label this subordinate a weak performer? Aren't there a few things that he does well? He must have displayed above-average qualifications when we decided to hire him. Did these qualifications evaporate all of a sudden?

The boss might even want to mentally play out part of the conversation beforehand. If I say this to the subordinate, what might he answer? Yes, sure, he would say that it was not his fault and that the customer was unreasonable. Those excuses—are they really without merit? Could he have a point? Could it be that, under other circumstances, I might have looked more favorably upon them? And if I still believe I'm right, how can I help the subordinate see things more clearly?

The boss must also mentally prepare himself to be open to the subordinate's views, even if the subordinate challenges him about any evidence regarding his poor performance. It will be easier for the boss to be open if, when preparing for the meeting, he has already challenged his own preconceptions.

Even when well prepared, bosses typically experience some degree of discomfort during intervention meetings. That is not all bad.

The subordinate will probably be somewhat uncomfortable as well, and it is reassuring for him to see that his boss is a human being, too.

Calculating Costs and Benefits

As we've said, an intervention is not always advisable. But when it is, it results in a range of outcomes that are uniformly better than the alternative—that is, continued underperformance and tension. After all, bosses who systematically choose either to ignore their subordinates' underperformance or to opt for the more expedient solution of simply removing perceived weak performers are condemned to keep repeating the same mistakes. Finding and training replacements for perceived weak performers is a costly and recurrent expense. So is monitoring and controlling the deteriorating performance of a disenchanted subordinate. Getting results *in spite of* one's staff is not a sustainable solution. In other words, it makes sense to think of the intervention as an investment, not an expense—with the payback likely to be high.

How high that payback will be and what form it will take obviously depend on the outcome of the intervention, which will itself depend not only on the quality of the intervention but also on several key contextual factors: How long has that relationship been spiraling downward? Does the subordinate have the intellectual and emotional resources to make the effort that will be required? Does the boss have enough time and energy to do his part?

We have observed outcomes that can be clustered into three categories. In the best-case scenario, the intervention leads to a mixture of coaching, training, job redesign, and a clearing of the air; as a result, the relationship and the subordinate's performance improve, and the costs associated with the syndrome go away or, at least, decrease measurably.

In the second-best scenario, the subordinate's performance improves only marginally, but because the subordinate received an honest and open hearing from the boss, the relationship between the two becomes more productive. Boss and subordinate develop a better understanding of those job dimensions the subordinate can do well and those he struggles with. This improved understanding leads the boss and the subordinate to explore *together* how they can develop a better fit between the job and the subordinate's strengths and weaknesses. That improved fit can be achieved by significantly modifying the subordinate's existing job or by transferring the subordinate to another job within the company. It may even result in the subordinate's choosing to leave the company.

While that outcome is not as successful as the first one, it is still productive; a more honest relationship eases the strain on both the boss and the subordinate, and in turn on the subordinate's subordinates. If the subordinate moves to a new job within the organization that better suits him, he will likely become a stronger performer. His relocation may also open up a spot in his old job for a better performer. The key point is that, having been treated fairly, the subordinate is much more likely to accept the outcome of the process. Indeed, recent studies show that the perceived fairness of a process has a major impact on employees' reactions to its outcomes. (See "Fair Process: Managing in the Knowledge Economy," by W. Chan Kim and Renée Mauborgne, HBR July–August 1997.)

Such fairness is a benefit even in the cases where, despite the boss's best efforts, neither the subordinate's performance nor his relationship with his boss improves significantly. Sometimes this happens: the subordinate truly lacks the ability to meet the job requirements, he has no interest in making the effort to improve, and the boss and the subordinate have both professional and personal differences that are irreconcilable. In those cases, however, the intervention still yields indirect benefits because, even if termination follows, other employees within the company are less likely to feel expendable or betrayed when they see that the subordinate received fair treatment.

Prevention Is the Best Medicine

The set-up-to-fail syndrome is not an organizational fait accompli. It can be unwound. The first step is for the boss to become aware of its existence and acknowledge the possibility that he might be part of the problem. The second step requires that the boss initiate a clear, focused intervention. Such an intervention demands an open exchange between the boss and the subordinate based on the evidence of poor performance, its underlying causes, and their joint responsibilities—culminating in a joint decision on how to work toward eliminating the syndrome itself.

Reversing the syndrome requires managers to challenge their own assumptions. It also demands that they have the courage to look within themselves for causes and solutions before placing the burden of responsibility where it does not fully belong. Prevention of the syndrome, however, is clearly the best option.

In our current research, we examine prevention directly. Our results are still preliminary, but it appears that bosses who manage to consistently avoid the set-up-to-fail syndrome have several traits in common. They do not, interestingly, behave the same way with all subordinates. They are more involved with some subordinates than others—they even monitor some subordinates more than others. However, they do so without disempowering and discouraging subordinates.

How? One answer is that those managers begin by being actively involved with all their employees, gradually reducing their involvement based on improved performance. Early guidance is not threatening to subordinates, because it is not triggered by performance shortcomings; it is systematic and meant to help set the conditions for future success. Frequent contact in the beginning of the relationship gives the boss ample opportunity to communicate with subordinates about priorities, performance measures, time allocation, and even expectations of the type and frequency of communication. That kind of clarity goes a long way toward preventing the dynamic of the set-up-to-fail syndrome, which is so often fueled by unstated expectations and a lack of clarity about priorities.

For example, in the case of Steve and Jeff, Jeff could have made explicit very early on that he wanted Steve to set up a system that would analyze the root causes of quality control rejections systematically. He could have explained the benefits of establishing such a system during the initial stages of setting up the new production line, and he might have expressed his intention to be actively involved in the system's design and early operation. His future involvement might then have decreased in such a way that could have been jointly agreed on at that stage.

Another way managers appear to avoid the set-up-to-fail syndrome is by challenging their own assumptions and attitudes about employees on an ongoing basis. They work hard at resisting the temptation to categorize employees in simplistic ways. They also monitor their own reasoning. For example, when feeling frustrated about a subordinate's performance, they ask themselves, "What are the facts?" They examine whether they are expecting things from the employee that have not been articulated, and they try to be objective about how often and to what extent the employee has really failed. In other words, these bosses delve into their own assumptions and behavior before they initiate a full-blown intervention.

Finally, managers avoid the set-up-to-fail syndrome by creating an environment in which employees feel comfortable discussing their performance and their relationships with the boss. Such an environment is a function of several factors: the boss's openness, his comfort level with having his own opinions challenged, even his sense of humor. The net result is that the boss and the subordinate feel free to communicate frequently and to ask one another questions about their respective behaviors before problems mushroom or ossify.

The methods used to head off the set-up-to-fail syndrome do, admittedly, involve a great deal of emotional investment from bosses—just as interventions do. We believe, however, that this higher emotional involvement is the key to getting subordinates to work to their full potential. As with most things in life, you can only expect to get a lot back if you put a lot in. As a senior executive once said to us, "The respect you give is the respect you get." We concur. If you want—indeed, need—the people in your organization to devote their whole hearts and minds to their work, then you must, too.

Originally published in March 1998. Reprint 98209.

Notes

1. *The influence of expectations on performance has been observed in numerous experiments by Dov Eden and his colleagues. See Dov Eden, "Leadership and Expectations: Pygmalion Effects and Other Self-fulfilling Prophecies in Organizations,"* Leadership Quarterly, *Winter 1992, vol. 3, no. 4, pp. 271–305.*

2. *Chris Argyris has written extensively on how and why people tend to behave unproductively in situations they see as threatening or embarrassing. See, for example,* Knowledge for Action: A Guide to Overcoming Barriers to Organizational Change *(San Francisco: Jossey-Bass, 1993).*

Saving Your Rookie Managers from Themselves

by Carol A. Walker

TOM EDELMAN, LIKE A million freshly minted managers before him, had done a marvelous job as an individual contributor. He was smart, confident, forward thinking, and resourceful. His clients liked him, as did his boss and coworkers. Consequently, no one in the department was surprised when his boss offered him a managerial position. Tom accepted with some ambivalence—he loved working directly with clients and was loath to give that up—but on balance, he was thrilled.

Six months later, when I was called into coach Tom (I've disguised his name), I had trouble even picturing the confident insider he once had been. He looked like a deer caught in the headlights. Tom seemed overwhelmed and indeed even used that word several times to describe how he felt. He had started to doubt his abilities. His direct reports, once close colleagues, no longer seemed to respect or even like him. What's more, his department had been beset by a series of small crises, and Tom spent most of his time putting out these fires. He knew this wasn't the most effective use of his time, but he didn't know how to stop. These problems hadn't yet translated into poor business results, but he was in trouble nonetheless.

His boss realized that he was in danger of failing and brought me in to assist. With support and coaching, Tom got the help he needed and eventually became an effective manager. Indeed, he has been promoted twice since I worked with him, and he now runs a small division within the same company. But his near failure—and the path that brought him to that point—is surprisingly typical. Most organizations promote employees into managerial positions based on their technical competence. Very often, however, those people fail to grasp how their roles have changed—that their jobs are no longer about personal achievement but instead about enabling others to achieve, that sometimes driving the bus means taking a backseat, and that building a team is often more important than cutting a deal. Even the best employees can have trouble adjusting to these new realities. That trouble may be exacerbated by normal insecurities that make rookie managers hesitant to ask for help, even when they find themselves in thoroughly unfamiliar territory. As these new managers internalize their stress, their focus becomes internal as well. They become insecure and self-focused and cannot properly support their teams. Inevitably, trust breaks down, staff members are alienated, and productivity suffers.

Many companies unwittingly support this downward spiral by assuming that their rookie managers will somehow learn critical management skills by osmosis. Some rookies do, to be sure, but in my experience they're the exceptions. Most need more help. In the absence of comprehensive training and intensive coaching—which most companies don't offer—the rookie manager's boss plays a key role. Of course, it's not possible for most senior managers to spend hours and hours every week overseeing a new manager's work, but if you know what typical challenges a rookie manager faces, you'll be able to anticipate some problems before they arise and nip others in the bud.

Delegating

Effective delegation may be one of the most difficult tasks for rookie managers. Senior managers bestow on them big responsibilities and tight deadlines, and they put a lot of pressure on them to produce

Idea in Brief

You've wisely promoted a top performer into management. Six months later, this rising star has fallen hard: He's overwhelmed, fearful, not respected by his staff. Why?

You probably promoted him based on his technical competence—then expected him to learn management skills by osmosis.

But he didn't grasp the real challenges of management—for example, empowering others versus striving for personal achievement. Insecure about asking for help, he turned inward. His team's morale plummeted; productivity faltered.

How to save your erstwhile star? Help him master delegating, thinking strategically, and communicating—basic skills that trip up *most* new managers.

results. The natural response of rookies when faced with such challenges is to "just do it," thinking that's what got them promoted in the first place. But their reluctance to delegate assignments also has its roots in some very real fears. First is the fear of losing stature: If I assign high-profile projects to my staff members, they'll get the credit. What kind of visibility will I be left with? Will it be clear to my boss and my staff what value I'm adding? Second is the fear of abdicating control: If I allow Frank to do this, how can I be sure that he will do it correctly? In the face of this fear, the rookie manager may delegate tasks but supervise Frank so closely that he will never feel accountable. Finally, the rookie may be hesitant to delegate work because he's afraid of overburdening his staff. He may be uncomfortable assigning work to former peers for fear that they'll resent him. But the real resentment usually comes when staff members feel that lack of opportunity is blocking their advancement.

Signs that these fears may be playing out include new managers who work excessively long hours, are hesitant to take on new responsibilities, have staff members who seem unengaged, or have a tendency to answer on behalf of employees instead of encouraging them to communicate with you directly.

The first step toward helping young managers delegate effectively is to get them to understand their new role. Acknowledge that

Idea in Practice

Essential management skills for rookie managers:

Delegating. Under pressure to produce, rookies often "just do it" themselves because they fear losing control or overburdening others. But failure to delegate blocks their staffs' advancement, making them resentful, and then disengaged.

How to help:

- Explain that developing staff is *as* essential as financial achievements.

- Lead by example. Trust and empower your rookie; he'll engage his *own* team.

- Encourage him to take small risks in playing to his staff's strengths. Early successes will build his confidence.

- Help him break complex projects into manageable chunks with clear milestones.

Getting support from above. Many rookie managers believe they're in servitude to bosses, not in partnership. To avoid seeming vulnerable, they don't ask for help. But if they don't see you as a critical support source, they won't see *themselves* as one for their team.

How to help:

- Emphasize that open communication is essential to your rookie's success. Discourage covering up problems.

- Introduce him to other managers as resources.

- Have *him* prepare agendas for your regular meetings. The process will help him organize his thoughts.

Projecting confidence. Rookies who don't project confidence won't energize their teams. Frantic, arrogant, or insecure demeanors may repel others in the company.

How to help:

- Encourage "conscious comportment": constant

their job fundamentally differs from an individual contributor's. Clarify what you and the organization value in leaders. Developing talented, promotable staff is critical in any company. Let new managers know that they will be rewarded for these less tangible efforts in addition to hitting numerical goals. Understanding this new role is half the battle for rookie managers, and one that many companies mistakenly assume is evident from the start.

awareness of the image your rookie is projecting.

- Let him express his feelings— but in your office, behind closed doors.

- Keep him from undermining his own authority; e.g., by pushing an initiative only because top management requested it. Walk through the process of presenting an initiative persuasively, ensuring he can *own* the message—not just deliver it.

Focusing on the big picture. Many rookie managers let fire fighting eclipse strategic initiatives. Fire fighting *feels* productive—but it doesn't teach teams to handle challenges themselves or think strategically.

How to help:

- Explain that strategic thinking will constitute more of your rookie's work as his career advances.

- Help him focus on the long-term, big picture. Ask strategic questions; e.g., "What market-place trends are you seeing that could affect you in six months?"

- Request written plans documenting strategic goals as well as concrete, supporting actions.

Giving constructive feedback. Most rookies dread correcting staffers' inadequate performance. But avoidance costs managers their credibility.

How to help:

- Explain that constructive feedback strengthens staffers' skills.

- Role-play giving feedback about behaviors, not personalities.

After clarifying how your rookie manager's role has changed, you can move on to tactics. Perhaps it goes without saying, but you should lead by example. You have the responsibility to empower the rookie who works for you and do what you can to help him over-come his insecurities about his value to the organization. You can then assist him in looking for opportunities to empower and engage his team.

One young manager I worked with desperately needed to find time to train and supervise new employees. His firm had been recently acquired, and he had to deal with high staff turnover and new industrywide rules and regulations. The most senior person on his staff—a woman who had worked for the acquiring company—was about to return from an extended family leave, and he was convinced that he couldn't ask her for help. After all, she had a part-time schedule, and she'd asked to be assigned to the company's largest client. To complicate matters, he suspected that she resented his promotion. As we evaluated the situation, the manager was able to see that the senior staffer's number one priority was reestablishing herself as an important part of the team. Once he realized this, he asked her to take on critical supervisory responsibilities, balanced with a smaller client load, and she eagerly agreed. Indeed, she returned from leave excited about partnering with her manager to develop the team.

When a new manager grumbles about mounting workloads, seize the opportunity to discuss delegation. Encourage him to take small risks initially, playing to the obvious strengths of his staff members. Asking his super-organized, reliable assistant to take the lead in handling the logistics of a new product launch, for example, is much less risky than asking a star salesperson, unaccustomed to this sort of detailed work, to do it. Early successes will build the manager's confidence and willingness to take progressively larger risks in stretching each team member's capabilities. Reinforce to him that delegation does not mean abdication. Breaking a complex project into manageable chunks, each with clearly defined milestones, makes effective follow-up easier. It's also important to schedule regular meetings before the project even begins in order to ensure that the manager stays abreast of progress and that staff members feel accountable.

Getting Support from Above

Most first-time managers see their relationship with their boss more as one of servitude than of partnership. They will wait for you to initiate meetings, ask for reports, and question results. You may welcome this restraint, but generally it's a bad sign. For one thing, it puts undue pressure on you to keep the flow of communication going. Even more important, it prevents new managers from looking to you as a critical source of support. If they don't see you that way, it's unlikely that they will see themselves that way for their own people. The problem isn't only that your position intimidates them; it's also that they fear being vulnerable. A newly promoted manager doesn't want you to see weaknesses, lest you think you made a mistake in promoting her. When I ask rookie managers about their relationships with their bosses, they often admit that they are trying to "stay under the boss's radar" and are "careful about what [they] say to the boss."

Some inexperienced managers will not seek your help even when they start to founder. Seemingly capable rookie managers often try to cover up a failing project or relationship—just until they can get it back under control. For example, one manager I worked with at a technology company hired a professional 20 years her senior. The transition was rocky, and, despite her best efforts, the individual wasn't acclimating to the organization. (The company, like many in the technology sector, was very youth oriented.) Rather than reaching out to her boss for help, the manager continued to grapple with the situation alone. The staff member ultimately resigned at the busiest time of the year, and the young manager suffered the dual punishment of being understaffed at the worst possible moment and having it known that she had lost a potentially important contributor.

What's the boss of a rookie manager to do? You can begin by clarifying expectations. Explain the connection between the rookie's success and your success, so that she understands that open communication is necessary for you to achieve your goals. Explain that you don't expect her to have all the answers. Introduce her to other managers within the company who may be helpful, and encourage her to contact them as needed. Let her know that mistakes happen but that the cover-up is always worse than the crime. Let her know that you like to receive occasional lunch invitations as much as you like to extend them.

Lunch and drop-by meetings are important, but they usually aren't enough. Consider meeting regularly with a new manager—perhaps weekly in the early stages of a new assignment, moving to biweekly or monthly as her confidence builds. These meetings will develop rapport, provide you with insight into how the person is approaching the job, and make the new manager organize her thoughts on a regular basis. Be clear that the meetings are her time and that it's up to her to plan the agenda. You're there to ask and answer questions and to offer advice. The message you send is that the individual's work is important to you and that you're a committed business partner. More subtly, you're modeling how to simultaneously empower and guide direct reports.

Projecting Confidence

Looking confident when you don't feel confident—it's a challenge we all face, and as senior managers we're usually conscious of the need when it arises. Rookie managers are often so internally focused that they are unaware of this need or the image they project. They are so focused on substance that they forget that form counts, too. The first weeks and months on the job are a critical time for new leaders to reach out to staff. If they don't project confidence, they are unlikely to inspire and energize their teams.

I routinely work with new managers who are unaware that their everyday demeanor is hurting their organizations. In one rapidly growing technology company, the service manager, Linda, faced high levels of stress. Service outages were all too common, and they were beyond her control. Customers were exacting, and they too were under great pressure. Her rapidly growing staff was generally inexperienced. Distraught customers and employees had her tied up in knots almost daily. She consistently appeared breathless, rushed, and fearful that the other shoe was about to drop. The challenge was perhaps too big for a first-time manager, but that's what happens in rapidly growing companies. On one level, Linda was doing an excellent job keeping the operation going. The client base was growing and retention was certainly high—largely as a result of her energy and resourcefulness. But on another level, she was doing a lot of damage.

Linda's frantic demeanor had two critical repercussions. First, she had unwittingly defined the standard for acceptable conduct in her department, and her inexperienced staff began to display the same behaviors. Before long, other departments were reluctant to communicate with Linda or her team, for fear of bothering them or eliciting an emotional reaction. But for the company to arrive at real solutions to the service problems, departments needed to openly exchange information, and that wasn't happening. Second, Linda was not portraying herself to senior managers as promotion material. They were pleased with her troubleshooting abilities, but they did not see a confident, thoughtful senior manager in the making. The image Linda was projecting would ultimately hold back both her career and her department.

Not all rookie managers display the problems that Linda did. Some appear excessively arrogant. Others wear their self-doubt on their sleeves. Whether your managers appear overwhelmed, arrogant, or insecure, honest feedback is your best tool. You can help rookie managers by telling them that it's always safe to let out their feelings—in your office, behind closed doors. Reinforce just how long a shadow they cast once they assume leadership positions. Their staff members watch them closely, and if they see professionalism and optimism, they are likely to demonstrate those characteristics as well. Preach the gospel of conscious comportment—a constant awareness of the image one is projecting to the world. If you observe a manager projecting a less-than-positive image, tell that person right away.

You should also be alert to new managers who undermine their own authority. Linda made another classic rookie mistake when she attempted to get her staff members to implement an initiative that her boss had come up with. In presenting the initiative, she let her team know it was important to implement because it had come from the division's senior vice president. While her intentions were good—rallying the team to perform—her words encouraged the group to focus attention above her rather than on her. There is no quicker way for a rookie manager to lose credibility with her staff than to appear to be a mouthpiece for senior management. Pointing out that senior management will be checking up on the initiative certainly won't hurt, but the rookie manager must take care never to be perceived simply as the messenger.

Just-in-time coaching is often the most effective method for showing rookie managers how to project confidence. For instance, the first time you ask a new manager to carry out an initiative, take a little extra time to walk her through the process. Impress upon her the cardinal rule of management: Your staff members don't necessarily have to like you, but they do need to trust you. Ensure that the new manager owns the message she's delivering.

Layoffs are a classic example of a message the rookie manager will struggle with. Don't allow a rookie to proceed half-prepared. Share as much information as you can. Make sure she's ready for all the likely questions and reactions by asking her to do an informal dry run with you. You might be surprised by how poorly she conveys the message in her first few attempts. A little practice may preserve the image of your manager and your company.

Focusing on the Big Picture

Rookie managers have a real knack for allowing immediate tasks to overshadow overarching initiatives. This is particularly true for those promoted from within, because they've just come from the front lines where they're accustomed to constant fire fighting. As a recent individual contributor armed with plenty of technical know-how, the rookie manager instinctively runs to the immediate rescue of any client or staff member in need. The sense of accomplishment rookies get from such rescues is seductive and far more exhilarating than rooting out the cause of all the fire fighting. And what could be better for team spirit than having the boss jump into the trenches and fight the good fight?

Of course, a leader shows great team spirit if he joins the troops in emergencies. But are all those emergencies true emergencies? Are newer staff members being empowered to handle complex challenges? And if the rookie manager is busy fighting fires, who is thinking strategically for the department? If you're the senior manager and these questions are popping into your head, you may well have a rookie manager who doesn't fully understand his role or is afraid to seize it.

I recently worked with a young manager who had become so accustomed to responding to a steady flow of problems that he was reluctant to block off any time to work on the strategic initiatives we had identified. When I probed, he revealed that he felt a critical part of his role was to wait for crises to arise. "What if I schedule this time and something urgent comes up and I disappoint someone?" he asked. When I pointed out that he could always postpone his strategy sessions if a true emergency arose, he seemed relieved. But he saw the concept of making time to think about the business as self-indulgent—this, despite the fact that his group was going to be asked to raise productivity significantly in the following fiscal year, and he'd done nothing to prepare for that reality.

Senior managers can help rookies by explaining to them that strategic thinking is a necessary skill for career advancement: For first-time managers, 10% of the work might be strategic and 90% tactical. As executives climb the corporate ladder, however, those percentages will flip-flop. To be successful at the next level, managers must demonstrate that they can think and act strategically. You can use your regularly scheduled meetings to help your managers focus on the big picture. Don't allow them to simply review the latest results and move on. Ask probing questions about those results. For example, "What trends are you seeing in the marketplace that could affect you in two quarters? Tell me how your competition is responding to those same trends." Don't let them regale you with the wonderful training their staffs have been getting without asking, "What additional skills do we need to build in the staff to increase productivity by 25% next year?" If you aren't satisfied with your managers' responses, let them know that you expect them to think this way—not to have all the answers, but to be fully engaged in the strategic thought process.

Rookie managers commonly focus on activities rather than on goals. That's because activities can be accomplished quickly (for example, conducting a seminar to improve the sales staff's presentation skills), whereas achieving goals generally takes more time (for example, actually enhancing the sales staff's effectiveness). The senior manager can help the rookie manager think strategically by asking for written goals that clearly distinguish between the goals and their supporting activities. Insisting on a goal-setting discipline will help your new (and not-so-new) managers to organize their strategic game plans. Critical but soft goals, such as staff development, are often overlooked because they are difficult to measure. Putting such goals in print with clear action steps makes them concrete, rendering a sense of accomplishment when they are achieved and a greater likelihood that they will be rewarded. Managers with clear goals will be less tempted to become full-time tacticians. Just as important, the process will help you ensure that they are thinking about the right issues and deploying their teams effectively.

Giving Constructive Feedback

It's human nature to avoid confrontations, and most people feel awkward when they have to correct others' behavior or actions. Rookie managers are no exception, and they often avoid addressing important issues with their staff. The typical scenario goes something like this: A staff member is struggling to meet performance goals or is acting inappropriately in meetings. The manager sits back, watches, and hopes that things will magically improve. Other staff members observe the situation and become frustrated by the manager's inaction. The manager's own frustration builds, as she can't believe the subordinate doesn't get it. The straightforward performance issue has now evolved into a credibility problem. When the manager finally addresses the problem, she personalizes it, lets her frustration seep into the discussion with her staff member, and finds the recipient rushing to defend himself from attack.

Most inexperienced managers wait far too long to talk with staff about performance problems. The senior manager can help by creating an environment in which constructive feedback is perceived not as criticism but as a source of empowerment. This begins with the feedback you offer to your managers about their own development. It can be as simple as getting them to tell you where their weaknesses are before they become problematic. After a good performance review, for example, you might say to your new manager, "By all accounts, you have a bright future here, so it's important that we talk about what you *don't* want me to know. What are you feeling least confident about? How can we address those areas so that you're ready for any opportunity that arises?" You'll probably be surprised by how attuned most high performers are to their own development needs. But they are not likely to do much about them unless you put those needs on the table.

More than likely, the feedback your managers have to offer their staffs will not always be so positive or easy to deliver. The key is to foster in them the desire to help their reports achieve their goals. Under those circumstances, even loathsome personal issues become approachable.

One of my clients managed a high-performing senior staff member who was notably unhelpful to others in the department and who resented her own lack of advancement. Instead of avoiding the issue because he didn't want to tell the staff member that she had a bad attitude, the senior manager took a more productive approach. He leveraged his knowledge of her personal goals to introduce the feedback. "I know that you're anxious for your first management role, and one of my goals is to help you attain that. I can't do that unless I'm completely honest with you. A big part of management is developing stronger skills in your staff. You aren't demonstrating that you enjoy that role. How can we can work together on that?" No guilt, no admonishment—just an offer to help her get what she wanted. Yet the message was received loud and clear.

A brainstorming session this client and I had about ways to offer critical feedback led to that approach. Often, brainstorming sessions can help rookie managers see that sticky personal issues can be broken down into straightforward business issues. In the case of the unhelpful senior staff member, her attitude didn't really need to enter the discussion; her actions did. Recommending a change in action is much easier than recommending a change in attitude. Never forget the old saw: You can't ask people to change their personalities, but you can ask them to change their behaviors.

Indeed, senior managers should share their own techniques for dealing with difficult conversations. One manager I worked with became defensive whenever a staff member questioned her judgment. She didn't really need me to tell her that her behavior was undermining her image and effectiveness. She did need me to offer her some techniques that would enable her to respond differently in the heat of the moment. She trained herself to respond quickly and earnestly with a small repertoire of questions like, "Can you tell me more about what you mean by that?" This simple technique bought her the time she needed to gather her thoughts and engage in an interchange that was productive rather than defensive. She was too close to the situation to come up with the technique herself.

Delegating, thinking strategically, communicating—you may think this all sounds like Management 101. And you're right. The most basic elements of management are often what trip up managers early in their careers. And because they are the basics, the bosses of rookie managers often take them for granted. They shouldn't—an extraordinary number of people fail to develop these skills. I've maintained an illusion throughout this article—that only rookie managers suffer because they haven't mastered these core skills. But the truth is, managers at all levels make these mistakes. An organization that supports its new managers by helping them to develop these skills will have surprising advantages over the competition.

Originally published in April 2002. Reprint R0204H.

What Great Managers Do

by Marcus Buckingham

"THE BEST BOSS I EVER HAD." That's a phrase most of us have said or heard at some point, but what does it mean? What sets the great boss apart from the average boss? The literature is rife with provocative writing about the qualities of managers and leaders and whether the two differ, but little has been said about what happens in the thousands of daily interactions and decisions that allows managers to get the best out of their people and win their devotion. What do great managers actually *do*?

In my research, beginning with a survey of 80,000 managers conducted by the Gallup Organization and continuing during the past two years with in-depth studies of a few top performers, I've found that while there are as many styles of management as there are managers, there is one quality that sets truly great managers apart from the rest: They discover what is unique about each person and then capitalize on it. Average managers play checkers, while great managers play chess. The difference? In checkers, all the pieces are uniform and move in the same way; they are interchangeable. You need to plan and coordinate their movements, certainly, but they all move at the same pace, on parallel paths. In chess, each type of piece moves in a different way, and you can't play if you don't know how each piece moves. More important, you won't win if you don't think carefully about how you move the pieces. Great managers know and value the unique abilities and even the eccentricities of their employees, and they learn how best to integrate them into a coordinated plan of attack.

This is the exact opposite of what great leaders do. Great leaders discover what is universal and capitalize on it. Their job is to rally people toward a better future. Leaders can succeed in this only when they can cut through differences of race, sex, age, nationality, and personality and, using stories and celebrating heroes, tap into those very few needs we all share. The job of a manager, meanwhile, is to turn one person's particular talent into performance. Managers will succeed only when they can identify and deploy the differences among people, challenging each employee to excel in his or her own way. This doesn't mean a leader can't be a manager or vice versa. But to excel at one or both, you must be aware of the very different skills each role requires.

The Game of Chess

What does the chess game look like in action? When I visited Michelle Miller, the manager who opened Walgreens' 4,000th store, I found the wall of her back office papered with work schedules. Michelle's store in Redondo Beach, California, employs people with sharply different skills and potentially disruptive differences in personality. A critical part of her job, therefore, is to put people into roles and shifts that will allow them to shine—and to avoid putting clashing personalities together. At the same time, she needs to find ways for individuals to grow.

There's Jeffrey, for example, a "goth rocker" whose hair is shaved on one side and long enough on the other side to cover his face. Michelle almost didn't hire him because he couldn't quite look her in the eye during his interview, but he wanted the hard-to-cover night shift, so she decided to give him a chance. After a couple of months, she noticed that when she gave Jeffrey a vague assignment, such as "Straighten up the merchandise in every aisle," what should have been a two-hour job would take him all night—and wouldn't be done very well. But if she gave him a more specific task, such as "Put up all

Idea in Brief

You've spent months coaching that employee to treat customers better, work more independently, or get organized—all to no avail.

How to make better use of your precious time? Do what great managers do: Instead of trying to change your employees, identify their unique abilities (and even their eccentricities)—then help them use those qualities to excel in their own way.

You'll need these three tactics:

- **Continuously tweak roles to capitalize on individual strengths.** One Walgreens store manager put a laconic but highly organized employee in charge of restocking aisles—freeing up more sociable employees to serve customers.

- **Pull the triggers that activate employees' strengths.** Offer incentives such as time spent with you, opportunities to work independently, and recognition in forms each employee values most.

- **Tailor coaching to unique learning styles.** Give "analyzers" the information they need before starting a task. Start "doers" off with simple tasks, then gradually raise the bar. Let "watchers" ride shotgun with your most experienced performers.

The payoff for capitalizing on employees' unique strengths? You save time. Your people take ownership for improving their skills. And you teach employees to value differences—building a powerful sense of team.

the risers for Christmas," all the risers would be symmetrical, with the right merchandise on each one, perfectly priced, labeled, and "faced" (turned toward the customer). Give Jeffrey a generic task, and he would struggle. Give him one that forced him to be accurate and analytical, and he would excel. This, Michelle concluded, was Jeffrey's forte. So, as any good manager would do, she told him what she had deduced about him and praised him for his good work.

And a good manager would have left it at that. But Michelle knew she could get more out Jeffrey. So she devised a scheme to reassign responsibilities across the entire store to capitalize on his unique strengths. In every Walgreens, there is a responsibility called "resets and revisions." A reset involves stocking an aisle with new merchandise, a task that usually coincides with a predictable change in

Idea in Practice

A closer look at the three tactics:

Capitalize on Employees' Strengths

First identify each employee's unique strengths: Walk around, observing people's reactions to events. Note activities each employee is drawn to. Ask "What was the best day at work you've had in the past three months?" Listen for activities people find intrinsically satisfying.

Watch for weaknesses, too, but downplay them in your communications with employees. Offer training to help employees overcome shortcomings stemming from lack of skills or knowledge. Otherwise, apply these strategies:

- **Find the employee a partner with complementary talents.** A merchandising manager who couldn't start tasks without exhaustive information performed superbly once her supervisor (the VP) began acting as her "information partner." The VP committed to leaving the manager a brief voicemail update daily and arranging two "touch base" conversations weekly.

- **Reconfigure work to neutralize weaknesses.** Use your creativity to envision more effective work arrangements, and be courageous about adopting unconventional job designs.

Activate Employees' Strengths

The ultimate trigger for activating an employee's strengths is recognition. But each employee plays to a different audience. So tailor your praise accordingly.

customer buying patterns (at the end of summer, for example, the stores will replace sun creams and lip balms with allergy medicines). A revision is a less time-consuming but more frequent version of the same thing: Replace these cartons of toothpaste with this new and improved variety. Display this new line of detergent at this end of the row. Each aisle requires some form of revision at least once a week.

In most Walgreens stores, each employee "owns" one aisle, where she is responsible not only for serving customers but also for

If an employee values recognition from...	Praise him by...
His peers	• Publicly celebrating his achievement in front of coworkers
You	• Telling him privately but vividly why he's such a valuable team member
Others with similar expertise	• Giving him a professional or technical award
Customers	• Posting a photo of him and his best customer in the office

Tailor Coaching to Learning Style

Adapt your coaching efforts to each employee's unique learning style:

If an employee is...	Coach him by...
An "**analyzer**"—he requires extensive information before taking on a task, and he hates making mistakes	• Giving him ample classroom time • Role-playing with him • Giving him time to prepare for challenges
A "**doer**"—he uses trial and error to enhance his skills while grappling with tasks	• Assigning him a simple task, explaining the desired outcomes, and getting out of his way • Gradually increasing a task's complexity until he masters his role
A "**watcher**"—he hones his skills by watching other people in action	• Having him "shadow" top performers.

facing the merchandise, keeping the aisle clean and orderly, tagging items with a Telxon gun, and conducting all resets and revisions. This arrangement is simple and efficient, and it affords each employee a sense of personal responsibility. But Michelle decided that since Jeffrey was so good at resets and revisions—and didn't enjoy interacting with customers—this should be his full-time job, in every single aisle.

It was a challenge. One week's worth of revisions requires a binder three inches thick. But Michelle reasoned that not only would

Jeffrey be excited by the challenge and get better and better with practice, but other employees would be freed from what they considered a chore and have more time to greet and serve customers. The store's performance proved her right. After the reorganization, Michelle saw not only increases in sales and profit but also in that most critical performance metric, customer satisfaction. In the subsequent four months, her store netted perfect scores in Walgreens' mystery shopper program.

So far, so very good. Sadly, it didn't last. This "perfect" arrangement depended on Jeffrey remaining content, and he didn't. With his success at doing resets and revisions, his confidence grew, and six months into the job, he wanted to move into management. Michelle wasn't disappointed by this, however; she was intrigued. She had watched Jeffrey's progress closely and had already decided that he might do well as a manager, though he wouldn't be a particularly emotive one. Besides, like any good chess player, she had been thinking a couple of moves ahead.

Over in the cosmetics aisle worked an employee named Genoa. Michelle saw Genoa as something of a double threat. Not only was she adept at putting customers at ease—she remembered their names, asked good questions, was welcoming yet professional when answering the phone—but she was also a neatnik. The cosmetics department was always perfectly faced, every product remained aligned, and everything was arranged just so. Her aisle was sexy: It made you want to reach out and touch the merchandise.

To capitalize on these twin talents, and to accommodate Jeffrey's desire for promotion, Michelle shuffled the roles within the store once again. She split Jeffrey's reset and revision job in two and gave the "revision" part of it to Genoa so that the whole store could now benefit from her ability to arrange merchandise attractively. But Michelle didn't want the store to miss out on Genoa's gift for customer service, so Michelle asked her to focus on the revision role only between 8:30 AM and 11 AM, and after that, when the store began to fill with customers on their lunch breaks, Genoa should shift her focus over to them.

She kept the reset role with Jeffrey. Assistant managers don't usually have an ongoing responsibility in the store, but, Michelle reasoned, he was now so good and so fast at tearing an aisle apart and rebuilding it that he could easily finish a major reset during a five-hour stint, so he could handle resets along with his managerial responsibilities.

By the time you read this, the Jeffrey–Genoa configuration has probably outlived its usefulness, and Michelle has moved on to design other effective and inventive configurations. The ability to keep tweaking roles to capitalize on the uniqueness of each person is the essence of great management.

A manager's approach to capitalizing on differences can vary tremendously from place to place. Walk into the back office at another Walgreens, this one in San Jose, California, managed by Jim Kawashima, and you won't see a single work schedule. Instead, the walls are covered with sales figures and statistics, the best of them circled with red felt-tip pen, and dozens of photographs of sales contest winners, most featuring a customer service representative named Manjit.

Manjit outperforms her peers consistently. When I first heard about her, she had just won a competition in Walgreens' suggestive selling program to sell the most units of Gillette deodorant in a month. The national average was 300; Manjit had sold 1,600. Disposable cameras, toothpaste, batteries—you name it, she could sell it. And Manjit won contest after contest despite working the graveyard shift, from 12:30 AM to 8:30 AM, during which she met significantly fewer customers than did her peers.

Manjit hadn't always been such an exceptional performer. She became stunningly successful only when Jim, who has made a habit of resuscitating troubled stores, came on board. What did Jim do to initiate the change in Manjit? He quickly picked up on her idiosyncrasies and figured out how to translate them into outstanding performance. For example, back in India, Manjit was an athlete—a runner and a weight lifter—and had always thrilled to the challenge of measured performance. When I interviewed her, one of the first

The Research

TO GATHER THE RAW MATERIAL for my book *The One Thing You Need to Know: About Great Managing, Great Leading, and Sustained Individual Success,* from which this article has been adapted, I chose an approach that is rather different from the one I used for my previous books. For 17 years, I had the good fortune to work with the Gallup Organization, one of the most respected research firms in the world. During that time, I was given the opportunity to interview some of the world's best leaders, managers, teachers, salespeople, stockbrokers, lawyers, and public servants. These interviews were a part of large-scale studies that involved surveying groups of people in the hopes of finding broad patterns in the data. For my book, I used this foundation as the jumping-off point for deeper, more individualized research.

In each of the three areas targeted in the book—managing, leading, and sustained individual success—I first identified one or two people in various roles and fields who had measurably, consistently, and dramatically outperformed their peers. These individuals included Myrtle Potter, president of commercial operations for Genentech, who transformed a failing drug into the highest selling prescription drug in the world; Sir Terry Leahy, the president of the European retailing giant Tesco; Manjit, the customer service representative

things out of her mouth was, "On Saturday, I sold 343 low-carb candy bars. On Sunday, I sold 367. Yesterday, 110, and today, 105." I asked if she always knows how well she's doing. "Oh yes," she replied. "Every day I check Mr. K's charts. Even on my day off, I make a point to come in and check my numbers."

Manjit loves to win and revels in public recognition. Hence, Jim's walls are covered with charts and figures, Manjit's scores are always highlighted in red, and there are photos documenting her success. Another manager might have asked Manjit to curb her enthusiasm for the limelight and give someone else a chance. Jim found a way to capitalize on it.

But what about Jim's other staff members? Instead of being resentful of Manjit's public recognition, the other employees came to understand that Jim took the time to see them as individuals and evaluate them based on their personal strengths. They also knew that Manjit's success spoke well of the entire store, so her success galvanized the team. In fact, before long, the pictures of Manjit from Jim Kawashima's top-performing Walgreens store in San Jose, California, who sold more than 1,600 units of Gillette deodorant in one month; and David Koepp, the prolific screenwriter who penned such blockbusters as *Jurassic Park, Mission: Impossible,* and *Spider-Man.*

What interested me about these high achievers was the practical, seemingly banal details of their actions and their choices. Why did Myrtle Potter repeatedly turn down promotions before taking on the challenge of turning around that failing drug? Why did Terry Leahy rely more on the memories of his working-class upbringing to define his company's strategy than on the results of customer surveys or focus groups? Manjit works the night shift, and one of her hobbies is weight lifting. Are those factors relevant to her performance? What were these special people doing that made them so very good at their roles?

Once these many details were duly noted and recorded, they slowly came together to reveal the "one thing" at the core of great managing, great leading, and sustained individual success.

began to include other employees from the store, too. After a few months, the San Jose location was ranked number one out of 4,000 in Walgreens' suggestive selling program.

Great Managers Are Romantics

Think back to Michelle. Her creative choreography may sound like a last resort, an attempt to make the best of a bad hire. It's not. Jeffrey and Genoa are not mediocre employees, and capitalizing on each person's uniqueness is a tremendously powerful tool.

First, identifying and capitalizing on each person's uniqueness saves time. No employee, however talented, is perfectly well-rounded. Michelle could have spent untold hours coaching Jeffrey and cajoling him into smiling at, making friends with, and remembering the names of customers, but she probably would have seen little result for her efforts. Her time was much better spent carving out a role that took advantage of Jeffrey's natural abilities.

The Elusive "One Thing"

IT'S BOLD TO CHARACTERIZE ANYTHING as *the* explanation or solution, so it's a risky move to make such definitive assertions as "this is the one thing all great managers do." But with enough research and focus, it is possible to identify that elusive "one thing."

I like to think of the concept of "one thing" as a "controlling insight." Controlling insights don't explain all outcomes or events; they serve as the best explanation of the greatest number of events. Such insights help you know which of your actions will have the most far-reaching influence in virtually every situation.

For a concept to emerge as the single controlling insight, it must pass three tests. First, it must be applicable across a wide range of situations. Take leadership as an example. Lately, much has been made of the notion that there is no one best way to lead and that instead, the most effective leadership style depends on the circumstance. While there is no doubt that different situations require different actions from a leader, that doesn't mean the most insightful thing you can say about leadership is that it's situational. With

Second, capitalizing on uniqueness makes each person more accountable. Michelle didn't just praise Jeffrey for his ability to execute specific assignments. She challenged him to make this ability the cornerstone of his contribution to the store, to take ownership for this ability, to practice it, and to refine it.

Third, capitalizing on what is unique about each person builds a stronger sense of team, because it creates interdependency. It helps people appreciate one anothers' particular skills and learn that their coworkers can fill in where they are lacking. In short, it makes people need one another. The old cliché is that there's no "I" in "team." But as Michael Jordan once said, "There may be no 'I' in 'team,' but there is in 'win.'"

Finally, when you capitalize on what is unique about each person, you introduce a healthy degree of disruption into your world. You shuffle existing hierarchies: If Jeffrey is in charge of all resets and revisions in the store, should he now command more or less respect than an assistant manager? You also shuffle existing assumptions about who is allowed to do what: If Jeffrey devises new methods of resetting enough focus, you can identify the one thing that underpins successful leadership across all situations and all styles.

Second, a controlling insight must serve as a multiplier. In any equation, some factors will have only an additive value: When you focus your actions on these factors, you see some incremental improvement. The controlling insight should be more powerful. It should show you how to get exponential improvement. For example, good managing is the result of a combination of many actions—selecting talented employees, setting clear expectations, catching people doing things right, and so on—but none of these factors qualifies as the "one thing" that great managers do, because even when done well, these actions merely prevent managers from chasing their best employees away.

Finally, the controlling insight must guide action. It must point to precise things that can be done to create better outcomes more consistently. Insights that managers can act on—rather than simply ruminate over—are the ones that can make all the difference.

an aisle, does he have to ask permission to try these out, or can he experiment on his own? And you shuffle existing beliefs about where the true expertise lies: If Genoa comes up with a way of arranging new merchandise that she thinks is more appealing than the method suggested by the "planogram" sent down from Walgreens headquarters, does her expertise trump the planners back at corporate? These questions will challenge Walgreens' orthodoxies and thus will help the company become more inquisitive, more intelligent, more vital, and, despite its size, more able to duck and weave into the future.

All that said, the reason great managers focus on uniqueness isn't just because it makes good business sense. They do it because they can't help it. Like Shelley and Keats, the nineteenth-century Romantic poets, great managers are fascinated with individuality for its own sake. Fine shadings of personality, though they may be invisible to some and frustrating to others, are crystal clear to and highly valued by great managers. They could no more ignore these subtleties than ignore their own needs and desires. Figuring out what makes people tick is simply in their nature.

The Three Levers

Although the Romantics were mesmerized by differences, at some point, managers need to rein in their inquisitiveness, gather up what they know about a person, and put the employee's idiosyncrasies to use. To that end, there are three things you must know about someone to manage her well: her strengths, the triggers that activate those strengths, and how she learns.

Make the most of strengths

It takes time and effort to gain a full appreciation of an employee's strengths and weaknesses. The great manager spends a good deal of time outside the office walking around, watching each person's reactions to events, listening, and taking mental notes about what each individual is drawn to and what each person struggles with. There's no substitute for this kind of observation, but you can obtain a lot of information about a person by asking a few simple, open-ended questions and listening carefully to the answers. Two queries in particular have proven most revealing when it comes to identifying strengths and weaknesses, and I recommend asking them of all new hires—and revisiting the questions periodically.

To identify a person's strengths, first ask, "What was the best day at work you've had in the past three months?" Find out what the person was doing and why he enjoyed it so much. Remember: A strength is not merely something you are good at. In fact, it might be something you aren't good at yet. It might be just a predilection, something you find so intrinsically satisfying that you look forward to doing it again and again and getting better at it over time. This question will prompt your employee to start thinking about his interests and abilities from this perspective.

To identify a person's weaknesses, just invert the question: "What was the worst day you've had at work in the past three months?" And then probe for details about what he was doing and why it grated on him so much. As with a strength, a weakness is not merely something you are bad at (in fact, you might be quite competent at it). It is something that drains you of energy, an activity that

What You Need to Know About Each of Your Direct Reports

- ☐ What are his or her strengths?
- ☐ What are the triggers that activate those strengths?
- ☐ What is his or her learning style?

you never look forward to doing and that when you are doing it, all you can think about is stopping.

Although you're keeping an eye out for both the strengths and weaknesses of your employees, your focus should be on their strengths. Conventional wisdom holds that self-awareness is a good thing and that it's the job of the manager to identify weaknesses and create a plan for overcoming them. But research by Albert Bandura, the father of social learning theory, has shown that self-assurance (labeled "self-efficacy" by cognitive psychologists), not self-awareness, is the strongest predictor of a person's ability to set high goals, to persist in the face of obstacles, to bounce back when reversals occur, and, ultimately, to achieve the goals they set. By contrast, self-awareness has not been shown to be a predictor of any of these outcomes, and in some cases, it appears to retard them.

Great managers seem to understand this instinctively. They know that their job is not to arm each employee with a dispassionately accurate understanding of the limits of her strengths and the liabilities of her weaknesses but to reinforce her self-assurance. That's why great managers focus on strengths. When a person succeeds, the great manager doesn't praise her hard work. Even if there's some exaggeration in the statement, he tells her that she succeeded because she has become so good at deploying her specific strengths. This, the manager knows, will strengthen the employee's self-assurance and make her more optimistic and more resilient in the face of challenges to come.

The focus-on-strengths approach might create in the employee a modicum of overconfidence, but great managers mitigate this by emphasizing the size and the difficulty of the employee's goals.

They know that their primary objective is to create in each employee a specific state of mind: one that includes a realistic assessment of the difficulty of the obstacle ahead but an unrealistically optimistic belief in her ability to overcome it.

And what if the employee fails? Assuming the failure is not attributable to factors beyond her control, always explain failure as a lack of effort, even if this is only partially accurate. This will obscure self-doubt and give her something to work on as she faces up to the next challenge.

Repeated failure, of course, may indicate weakness where a role requires strength. In such cases, there are four approaches for overcoming weaknesses. If the problem amounts to a lack of skill or knowledge, that's easy to solve: Simply offer the relevant training, allow some time for the employee to incorporate the new skills, and look for signs of improvement. If her performance doesn't get better, you'll know that the reason she's struggling is because she is missing certain talents, a deficit no amount of skill or knowledge training is likely to fix. You'll have to find a way to manage around this weakness and neutralize it.

Which brings us to the second strategy for overcoming an employee weakness. Can you find her a partner, someone whose talents are strong in precisely the areas where hers are weak? Here's how this strategy can look in action. As vice president of merchandising for the women's clothing retailer Ann Taylor, Judi Langley found that tensions were rising between her and one of her merchandising managers, Claudia (not her real name), whose analytical mind and intense nature created an overpowering "need to know." If Claudia learned of something before Judi had a chance to review it with her, she would become deeply frustrated. Given the speed with which decisions were made, and given Judi's busy schedule, this happened frequently. Judi was concerned that Claudia's irritation was unsettling the whole product team, not to mention earning the employee a reputation as a malcontent.

An average manager might have identified this behavior as a weakness and lectured Claudia on how to control her need for information.

Judi, however, realized that this "weakness" was an aspect of Claudia's greatest strength: her analytical mind. Claudia would never be able to rein it in, at least not for long. So Judi looked for a strategy that would honor and support Claudia's need to know, while channeling it more productively. Judi decided to act as Claudia's information partner, and she committed to leaving Claudia a voice mail at the end of each day with a brief update. To make sure nothing fell through the cracks, they set up two live "touch base" conversations per week. This solution managed Claudia's expectations and assured her that she would get the information she needed, if not exactly when she wanted it, then at least at frequent and predictable intervals. Giving Claudia a partner neutralized the negative manifestations of her strength, allowing her to focus her analytical mind on her work. (Of course, in most cases, the partner would need to be someone other than a manager.)

Should the perfect partner prove hard to find, try this third strategy: Insert into the employee's world a technique that helps accomplish through discipline what the person can't accomplish through instinct. I met one very successful screenwriter and director who had struggled with telling other professionals, such as composers and directors of photography, that their work was not up to snuff. So he devised a mental trick: He now imagines what the "god of art" would want and uses this imaginary entity as a source of strength. In his mind, he no longer imposes his own opinion on his colleagues but rather tells himself (and them) that an authoritative third party has weighed in.

If training produces no improvement, if complementary partnering proves impractical, and if no nifty discipline technique can be found, you are going to have to try the fourth and final strategy, which is to rearrange the employee's working world to render his weakness irrelevant, as Michelle Miller did with Jeffrey. This strategy will require of you, first, the creativity to envision a more effective arrangement and, second, the courage to make that arrangement work. But as Michelle's experience revealed, the payoff that may come in the form of increased employee productivity and engagement is well worth it.

Trigger good performance

A person's strengths aren't always on display. Sometimes they require precise triggering to turn them on. Squeeze the right trigger, and a person will push himself harder and persevere in the face of resistance. Squeeze the wrong one, and the person may well shut down. This can be tricky because triggers come in myriad and mysterious forms. One employee's trigger might be tied to the time of day (he is a night owl, and his strengths only kick in after 3 PM). Another employee's trigger might be tied to time with you, the boss (even though he's worked with you for more than five years, he still needs you to check in with him every day, or he feels he's being ignored). Another worker's trigger might be just the opposite—independence (she's only worked for you for six months, but if you check in with her even once a week, she feels micromanaged).

The most powerful trigger by far is recognition, not money. If you're not convinced of this, start ignoring one of your highly paid stars, and watch what happens. Most managers are aware that employees respond well to recognition. Great managers refine and extend this insight. They realize that each employee plays to a slightly different audience. To excel as a manager, you must be able to match the employee to the audience he values most. One employee's audience might be his peers; the best way to praise him would be to stand him up in front of his coworkers and publicly celebrate his achievement. Another's favorite audience might be you; the most powerful recognition would be a one-on-one conversation where you tell him quietly but vividly why he is such a valuable member of the team. Still another employee might define himself by his expertise; his most prized form of recognition would be some type of professional or technical award. Yet another might value feedback only from customers, in which case a picture of the employee with her best customer or a letter to her from the customer would be the best form of recognition.

Given how much personal attention it requires, tailoring praise to fit the person is mostly a manager's responsibility. But organizations can take a cue from this, too. There's no reason why a large company can't take this individualized approach to recognition and apply it to every employee. Of all the companies I've encountered, the North American division of HSBC, a London-based bank, has done the best job of this. Each year it presents its top individual consumer-lending performers with its Dream Awards. Each winner receives a unique prize. During the year, managers ask employees to identify what they would like to receive should they win. The prize value is capped at $10,000, and it cannot be redeemed as cash, but beyond those two restrictions, each employee is free to pick the prize he wants. At the end of the year, the company holds a Dream Awards gala, during which it shows a video about the winning employee and why he selected his particular prize.

You can imagine the impact these personalized prizes have on HSBC employees. It's one thing to be brought up on stage and given yet another plaque. It's another thing when, in addition to public recognition of your performance, you receive a college tuition fund for your child, or the Harley-Davidson motorcycle you've always dreamed of, or—the prize everyone at the company still talks about—the airline tickets to fly you and your family back to Mexico to visit the grandmother you haven't seen in ten years.

Tailor to learning styles

Although there are many learning styles, a careful review of adult learning theory reveals that three styles predominate. These three are not mutually exclusive; certain employees may rely on a combination of two or perhaps all three. Nonetheless, staying attuned to each employee's style or styles will help focus your coaching.

First, there's analyzing. Claudia from Ann Taylor is an analyzer. She understands a task by taking it apart, examining its elements, and reconstructing it piece by piece. Because every single component of a task is important in her eyes, she craves information. She needs to absorb all there is to know about a subject before she can begin to feel comfortable with it. If she doesn't feel she has enough information, she will dig and push until she gets it. She will read the assigned reading. She will attend the required classes. She will take good notes. She will study. And she will still want more.

The best way to teach an analyzer is to give her ample time in the classroom. Role-play with her. Do postmortem exercises with her. Break her performance down into its component parts so she can carefully build it back up. Always allow her time to prepare. The analyzer hates mistakes. A commonly held view is that mistakes fuel learning, but for the analyzer, this just isn't true. In fact, the reason she prepares so diligently is to minimize the possibility of mistakes. So don't expect to teach her much by throwing her into a new situation and telling her to wing it.

The opposite is true for the second dominant learning style, doing. While the most powerful learning moments for the analyzer occur prior to the performance, the doer's most powerful moments occur *during* the performance. Trial and error are integral to this learning process. Jeffrey, from Michelle Miller's store, is a doer. He learns the most while he's in the act of figuring things out for himself. For him, preparation is a dry, uninspiring activity. So rather than role-play with someone like Jeffrey, pick a specific task within his role that is simple but real, give him a brief overview of the outcomes you want, and get out of his way. Then gradually increase the degree of each task's complexity until he has mastered every aspect of his role. He may make a few mistakes along the way, but for the doer, mistakes are the raw material for learning.

Finally, there's watching. Watchers won't learn much through role-playing. They won't learn by doing, either. Since most formal training programs incorporate both of these elements, watchers are often viewed as rather poor students. That may be true, but they aren't necessarily poor learners.

Watchers can learn a great deal when they are given the chance to see the total performance. Studying the individual parts of a task is about as meaningful for them as studying the individual pixels of a digital photograph. What's important for this type of learner is the content of each pixel, its position relative to all the others. Watchers are only able to see this when they view the complete picture.

As it happens, this is the way I learn. Years ago, when I first began interviewing, I struggled to learn the skill of creating a report on a person after I had interviewed him. I understood all the required steps, but I couldn't seem to put them together. Some of my colleagues could knock out a report in an hour; for me, it would take the better part of a day. Then one afternoon, as I was staring morosely into my Dictaphone, I overheard the voice of the analyst next door. He was talking so rapidly that I initially thought he was on the phone. Only after a few minutes did I realize that he was dictating a report. This was the first time I had heard someone "in the act." I'd seen the finished results countless times, since reading the reports of others was the way we were supposed to learn, but I'd never actually heard another analyst in the act of creation. It was a revelation. I finally saw how everything should come together into a coherent whole. I remember picking up my Dictaphone, mimicking the cadence and even the accent of my neighbor, and feeling the words begin to flow.

If you're trying to teach a watcher, by far the most effective technique is to get her out of the classroom. Take her away from the manuals, and make her ride shotgun with one of your most experienced performers.

We've seen, in the stories of great managers like Michelle Miller and Judi Langley, that at the very heart of their success lies an appreciation for individuality. This is not to say that managers don't need other skills. They need to be able to hire well, to set expectations, and to interact productively with their own bosses, just to name a few. But what they do—instinctively—is play chess. Mediocre managers assume (or hope) that their employees will all be motivated by the same things and driven by the same goals, that they will desire the same kinds of relationships and learn in roughly the same way. They define the behaviors they expect from people and tell them to work on behaviors that don't come naturally. They praise those who can overcome their natural styles to conform to preset ideas. In short, they believe the manager's job is to mold, or transform, each employee into the perfect version of the role.

Great managers don't try to change a person's style. They never try to push a knight to move in the same way as a bishop. They know that their employees will differ in how they think, how they build relationships, how altruistic they are, how patient they can be, how much of an expert they need to be, how prepared they need to feel, what drives them, what challenges them, and what their goals are. These differences of trait and talent are like blood types: They cut across the superficial variations of race, sex, and age and capture the essential uniqueness of each individual.

Like blood types, the majority of these differences are enduring and resistant to change. A manager's most precious resource is time, and great managers know that the most effective way to invest their time is to identify exactly how each employee is different and then to figure out how best to incorporate those enduring idiosyncrasies into the overall plan.

To excel at managing others, you must bring that insight to your actions and interactions. Always remember that great managing is about release, not transformation. It's about constantly tweaking your environment so that the unique contribution, the unique needs, and the unique style of each employee can be given free rein. Your success as a manager will depend almost entirely on your ability to do this.

Originally published in March 2005. Reprint R0503D.

Fair Process

Managing in the Knowledge Economy. *by W. Chan Kim and Renée Mauborgne*

A LONDON POLICEMAN GAVE a woman a ticket for making an illegal turn. When the woman protested that there was no sign prohibiting the turn, the policeman pointed to one that was bent out of shape and difficult to see from the road. Furious, the woman decided to appeal by going to court. Finally, the day of her hearing arrived, and she could hardly wait to speak her piece. But she had just begun to tell her side of the story when the magistrate stopped her and summarily ruled in her favor.

How did the woman feel? Vindicated? Victorious? Satisfied?

No, she was frustrated and deeply unhappy. "I came for justice," she complained, "but the magistrate never let me explain what happened." In other words, although she liked the outcome, she didn't like the process that had created it.

For the purposes of their theories, economists assume that people are maximizers of utility, driven mainly by rational calculations of their own self-interest. That is, economists assume people focus solely on outcomes. That assumption has migrated into much of management theory and practice. It has, for instance, become embedded in the tools managers traditionally use to control and motivate employees' behavior—from incentive systems to organizational structures. But it is an assumption that managers would do well to reexamine because we all know that in real life it doesn't always hold true. People do care about outcomes, but—like the woman in London—they also care about the processes that produce those outcomes. They want to know that they had their say—that their point of view was considered even if it was rejected. Outcomes matter, but no more than the fairness of the processes that produce them.

Never has the idea of fair process been more important for managers than it is today. Fair process turns out to be a powerful management tool for companies struggling to make the transition from a production-based to a knowledge-based economy, in which value creation depends increasingly on ideas and innovation. Fair process profoundly influences attitudes and behaviors critical to high performance. It builds trust and unlocks ideas. With it, managers can achieve even the most painful and difficult goals while gaining the voluntary cooperation of the employees affected. Without fair process, even outcomes that employees might favor can be difficult to achieve—as the experience of an elevator manufacturer we'll call Elco illustrates.

Good Outcome, Unfair Process

In the late 1980s, sales in the elevator industry headed south as over-construction of office space left some large U.S. cities with vacancy rates as high as 20%. Faced with diminished domestic demand for its product, Elco knew it had to improve its operations. The company made the decision to replace its batch-manufacturing system with a cellular approach that would allow self-directed teams to achieve superior performance. Given the industry's collapse, top management felt the transformation had to be made in record time.

Lacking expertise in cellular manufacturing, Elco retained a consulting firm to design a master plan for the conversion. Elco asked the consultants to work quickly and with minimal disturbance to employees. The new manufacturing system would be installed first at Elco's Chester plant, where employee relations were so good that in 1983 workers had decertified their own union. Subsequently, Elco would roll the process out to its High Park plant, where a strong union would probably resist that, or any other, change.

Idea in Brief

In just months, a model workforce degenerated into a cauldron of mistrust, resistance, and plummeting performance. Why? Management launched a major change effort without inviting employees' input, without explaining the reasons for the change, and without clarifying new performance expectations.

In other words, the company ignored **fair process**—a decision-making approach that addresses our basic human need to be valued and respected. When people feel a decision affecting them was made fairly, they trust and cooperate with managers. They share ideas and willingly go beyond the call of duty. Corporate performance soars.

In knowledge-based organizations—whose lifeblood consists of employees' trust, commitment, and ideas—fair process is essential. It enables companies to channel people's energy and creativity toward organizational goals.

The benefits of fair process may seem obvious—yet most organizations don't practice it. Why? Some managers find it threatening, assuming it will diminish their power. They keep employees at arm's length to avoid challenges to their authority. Others believe employees are concerned only with what's best for themselves. But evidence shows that most people will accept outcomes not wholly in their favor—*if* they believe the process for arriving at those outcomes was fair.

Under the leadership of a much beloved plant manager, Chester was in all respects a model operation. Visiting customers were always impressed by the knowledge and enthusiasm of Chester's employees, so much so that the vice president of marketing saw the plant as one of Elco's best marketing tools. "Just let customers talk with Chester employees," he observed, "and they walk away convinced that buying an Elco elevator is the smart choice."

But one day in January of 1991, Chester's employees arrived at work to discover strangers at the plant. Who were these people wearing dark suits, white dress shirts, and ties? They weren't customers. They showed up daily and spoke in low tones to one another. They didn't interact with employees. They hovered behind people's backs, taking notes and drawing fancy diagrams. The rumor

Idea in Practice

Fair process isn't decision by consensus or democracy in the workplace. Its goal is to pursue the best ideas, not create harmony. Fair process consists of three principles:

- *Engagement*—involving individuals in decisions by inviting their input and encouraging them to challenge one another's ideas. Engagement communicates management's respect for individuals and their ideas and builds collective wisdom. It generates better decisions and greater commitment from those involved in executing those decisions.

- *Explanation*—clarifying the thinking behind a final decision. Explanation reassures people that managers have considered their opinions and made the decision with the company's overall interests at heart. Employees trust managers' intentions—even if their own ideas were rejected.

- *Expectation clarity*—stating the new rules of the game, including performance standards, penalties for failure, and new responsibilities. By minimizing political jockeying and favoritism, expectation clarity enables employees to focus on the job at hand.

Example: Facing decreasing demand, an elevator manufacturer we'll call Elco decided to design a more efficient manufacturing system. It would introduce the system at its Chester plant, a model operation with such positive employee relations that it decertified its own union. Then it would incorporate the new system at High Park, a strongly unionized plant highly resistant to change.

Seeking minimal workforce disturbance, managers didn't involve the Chester employees in the system design process, explain why change was necessary, or clarify new performance expectations. Soon rumors about layoffs proliferated, trust and commitment deteriorated, and fights erupted on the shop floor. Quality sank.

Rattled but wiser, Elco took a different tack at their High Park site. Managers held ongoing plantwide meetings to explain the need for the new system, encouraged employees to help design the new process, and laid out new expectations. The anticipated resistance never came—and trusting employees embraced the new system.

circulated that after employees went home in the afternoon, these people would swarm across the plant floor, snoop around people's workstations, and have heated discussions.

During this period, the plant manager was increasingly absent. He was spending more time at Elco's head office in meetings with the consultants—sessions deliberately scheduled away from the plant so as not to distract the employees. But the plant manager's absence produced the opposite effect. As people grew anxious, wondering why the captain of their ship seemed to be deserting them, the rumor mill moved into high gear. Everyone became convinced that the consultants would downsize the plant. They were sure they were about to lose their jobs. The fact that the plant manager was always gone—obviously, he was avoiding them—and that no explanation was given, could only mean that management was, they thought, "trying to pull one over on us." Trust and commitment at the Chester plant quickly deteriorated. Soon, people were bringing in newspaper clippings about other plants around the country that had been shut down with the help of consultants. Employees saw themselves as imminent victims of yet another management fad and resented it.

In fact, Elco managers had no intention of closing the plant. They wanted to cut out waste, freeing people to enhance quality and produce elevators for new international markets. But plant employees could not have known that.

The master plan

In March 1991, management gathered the Chester employees in a large room. Three months after the consultants had first appeared, they were formally introduced. At the same time, management unveiled to employees the master plan for change at the Chester plant. In a meeting that lasted only 30 minutes, employees heard how their time-honored way of working would be abolished and replaced by something called "cellular manufacturing." No one explained why the change was needed, nor did anyone say exactly what would be expected of employees under the new approach. The managers didn't mean to skirt the issues; they just didn't feel they had the time to go into details.

The employees sat in stunned silence, which the managers mistook for acceptance, forgetting how many months it had taken them as leaders to get comfortable with the idea of cellular manufacturing and the changes it entailed. The managers felt good when the meeting was over, believing the employees were on board. With such a terrific staff, they thought, implementation of the new system was bound to go well.

Master plan in hand, management quickly began rearranging the plant. When employees asked what the new layout aimed to achieve, the response was "efficiency gains." The managers didn't have time to explain why efficiency needed to be improved and didn't want to worry employees. But lacking an intellectual understanding of what was happening to them, some employees literally began feeling sick when they came to work.

Managers informed employees that they would no longer be judged on individual performance but rather on the performance of the cell. They said quicker or more experienced employees would have to pick up the slack for slower or less experienced colleagues. But they didn't elaborate. How the new system was supposed to work, management didn't make clear.

In fact, the new cell design offered tremendous benefits to employees, making vacations easier to schedule, for example, and giving them the opportunity to broaden their skills and engage in a greater variety of work. But lacking trust in the change process, employees could see only its negative side. They began taking out their fears and anger on one another. Fights erupted on the plant floor as employees refused to help those they called "lazy people who can't finish their own jobs" or interpreted offers of help as meddling, responding with, "This is my job. You keep to your own workstation."

Chester's model workforce was falling apart. For the first time in the plant manager's career, employees refused to do as they were asked, turning down assignments "even if you fire me." They felt they could no longer trust the once popular plant manager, so they began to go around him, taking their complaints directly to his boss at the head office.

The plant manager then announced that the new cell design would allow employees to act as self-directed teams and that the role of the supervisor would be abolished. He expected people to react with excitement to his vision of Chester as the epitome of the factory of the future, where employees are empowered as entrepreneurial agents. Instead, they were simply confused. They had no idea how to succeed in this new environment. Without supervisors, what would they do if stock ran short or machines broke down? Did empowerment mean that the teams could self-authorize overtime, address quality problems such as rework, or purchase new machine tools? Unclear about how to succeed, employees felt set up to fail.

Time out

By the summer of 1991, both cost and quality performance were in a free fall. Employees were talking about bringing the union back. Finally, in despair, the plant manager phoned Elco's industrial psychologist. "I need your help," he said. "I have lost control."

The psychologist conducted an employee opinion survey to learn what had gone wrong. Employees complained, "Management doesn't care about our ideas or our input." They felt that the company had scant respect for them as individuals, treating them as if they were not worthy of knowing about business conditions: "They don't bother to tell us where we are going and what this means to us." And they were deeply confused and mistrustful: "We don't know exactly what management expects of us in this new cell."

What Is Fair Process?

The theme of justice has preoccupied writers and philosophers throughout the ages, but the systematic study of fair process emerged only in the mid-1970s, when two social scientists, John W. Thibaut and Laurens Walker, combined their interest in the psychology of justice with the study of process. Focusing their attention on legal settings, they sought to understand what makes people trust a legal system so that they will comply with laws without being coerced into doing so. Their research established that people care as

Making Sense of Irrational Behavior at VW and Siemens-Nixdorf

Economic theories do a good job of explaining the rational side of human behavior, but they fall short in explaining why people can act negatively in the face of positive outcomes. Fair process offers managers a theory of behavior that explains—or might help predict—what would otherwise appear to be bewilderingly noneconomic, or irrational, behavior.

Consider what happened to Volkswagen. In 1992, the German carmaker was in the midst of expanding its manufacturing facility in Puebla, Mexico, its only production site in North America. The appreciation of the deutsche mark against the U.S. dollar was pricing Volkswagen out of the U.S. market. But after the North American Free Trade Agreement (NAFTA) became law in 1992, Volkswagen's cost-efficient Mexican facility was well positioned to reconquer the large North American market.

In the summer of 1992, a new labor agreement had to be hammered out. The accord VW signed with the union's secretary-general included a generous 20% pay raise for employees. VW thought the workers would be pleased.

But the union's leaders had not involved the employees in discussions about the contract's terms; they did a poor job of communicating what the new agreement would mean to employees and why a number of work-rule changes were necessary. Workers did not understand the basis for the decisions their leaders had taken. They felt betrayed.

VW's management was completely caught off guard when, on July 21, the employees started a massive walkout that cost the company as much as an estimated $10 million per day. On August 21, about 300 protesters were attacked by police dogs. The government was forced to step in to end the violence. Volkswagen's plans for the U.S. market were in disarray, and its performance was devastated.

In contrast, consider the turnaround of Siemens-Nixdorf Informationssysteme (SNI), the largest European supplier of information technology. Created in 1990 when Siemens acquired the troubled Nixdorf Computer Company, SNI had cut head count from 52,000 to 35,000 by 1994. Anxiety and fear were rampant at the company.

In 1994, Gerhard Schulmeyer, the newly appointed CEO, went out to talk to as many employees as he could. In a series of meetings large and small with a total of more than 11,000 people, Schulmeyer shared his crusading mission to engage everyone in turning the company around. He began by painting a bleakly honest picture of SNI's situation: The company was losing money despite recent efforts to slash costs. Deeper cuts were needed, and every business would have to demonstrate its viability or be eliminated. Schulmeyer set clear but tough rules about how decisions would be made. He then asked for volunteers to come up with ideas.

Within three months, the initial group of 30 volunteers grew to encompass an additional 75 SNI executives and 300 employees. These 405 change agents soon turned into 1,000, then 3,000, then 9,000, as they progressively recruited others to help save the company. Throughout the process, ideas were solicited from managers and employees alike concerning decisions that affected them, and they all understood how decisions would be made. Ideas would be auctioned off to executives willing to champion and finance them. If no executive bought a proposal on its merits, the idea would not be pursued. Although 20% to 30% of their proposals were rejected, employees thought the process was fair.

People voluntarily pitched in—mostly after business hours, often until midnight. In just over two years, SNI has achieved a transformation notable in European corporate history. Despite accumulated losses of DM 2 billion, by 1995 SNI was already operating in the black. In the same period, employee satisfaction almost doubled, despite the radical and difficult changes under way.

Why did employees of Volkswagen revolt, despite their upbeat economic circumstances? How, in the face of such demoralizing economic conditions, could SNI turn around its performance? What is at issue is not *what* the two companies did but *how* they did it. The cases illustrate the tremendous power of fair process—fairness in the process of making and executing decisions. Fair process profoundly influences attitudes and behavior critical to high performance.

much about the fairness of the process through which an outcome is produced as they do about the outcome itself. Subsequent researchers such as Tom R. Tyler and E. Allan Lind demonstrated the power of fair process across diverse cultures and social settings.

We discovered the managerial relevance of fair process more than a decade ago, during a study of strategic decision making in multinational corporations. Many top executives in those corporations were frustrated—and baffled—by the way the senior managers of their local subsidiaries behaved. Why did those managers so often fail to share information and ideas with the executives? Why did they sabotage the execution of plans they had agreed to carry out? In the 19 companies we studied, we found a direct link between processes, attitudes, and behavior. Managers who believed the company's processes were fair displayed a high level of trust and commitment, which, in turn, engendered active cooperation. Conversely, when managers felt fair process was absent, they hoarded ideas and dragged their feet.

In subsequent field research, we explored the relevance of fair process in other business contexts—for example, in companies in the midst of transformations, in teams engaged in product innovation, and in company-supplier partnerships. (See the sidebar "Making Sense of Irrational Behavior at VW and Siemens-Nixdorf.") For companies seeking to harness the energy and creativity of committed managers and employees, the central idea that emerges from our fair-process research is this: Individuals are most likely to trust and cooperate freely with systems—whether they themselves win or lose by those systems—when fair process is observed.

Fair process responds to a basic human need. All of us, whatever our role in a company, want to be valued as human beings and not as "personnel" or "human assets." We want others to respect our intelligence. We want our ideas to be taken seriously. And we want to understand the rationale behind specific decisions. People are sensitive to the signals conveyed through a company's decision-making processes. Such processes can reveal a company's willingness to trust people and seek their ideas—or they can signal the opposite.

The three principles

In all the diverse management contexts we have studied, we have asked people to identify the bedrock elements of fair process. And whether we were working with senior executives or shop floor employees, the same three mutually reinforcing principles consistently emerged: engagement, explanation, and expectation clarity.

Engagement means involving individuals in the decisions that affect them by asking for their input and allowing them to refute the merits of one another's ideas and assumptions. Engagement communicates management's respect for individuals and their ideas. Encouraging refutation sharpens everyone's thinking and builds collective wisdom. Engagement results in better decisions by management and greater commitment from all involved in executing those decisions.

Explanation means that everyone involved and affected should understand why final decisions are made as they are. An explanation of the thinking that underlies decisions makes people confident that managers have considered their opinions and have made those decisions impartially in the overall interests of the company. An explanation allows employees to trust managers' intentions even if their own ideas have been rejected. It also serves as a powerful feedback loop that enhances learning.

Expectation clarity requires that once a decision is made, managers state clearly the new rules of the game. Although the expectations may be demanding, employees should know up front by what standards they will be judged and the penalties for failure. What are the new targets and milestones? Who is responsible for what? To achieve fair process, it matters less what the new rules and policies are and more that they are clearly understood. When people clearly understand what is expected of them, political jockeying and favoritism are minimized, and they can focus on the job at hand.

Notice that fair process is not decision by consensus. Fair process does not set out to achieve harmony or to win people's support through compromises that accommodate every individual's opinions, needs, or interests. While fair process gives every idea a chance, the merit of the ideas—and not consensus—is what drives the decision making.

Nor is fair process the same as democracy in the workplace. Achieving fair process does not mean that managers forfeit their prerogative to make decisions and establish policies and procedures. Fair process pursues the best ideas whether they are put forth by one or many.

"We really screwed up"

Elco managers violated all three basic principles of fair process at the Chester plant. They failed to engage employees in decisions that directly affected them. They didn't explain why decisions were being made the way they were and what those decisions meant to employees' careers and work methods. And they neglected to make clear what would be expected of employees under cellular manufacturing. In the absence of fair process, the employees at Chester rejected the transformation.

A week after the psychologist's survey was completed, management invited employees to meetings in groups of 20. Employees surmised that management was either going to pretend that the survey had never happened or accuse employees of disloyalty for having voiced their complaints. But to their amazement, managers kicked off the meeting by presenting the undiluted survey results and declaring, "We were wrong. We really screwed up. In our haste and ignorance, we did not go through the proper process." Employees couldn't believe their ears. There were whispers in the back of the room, "What the devil did they say?" At more than 20 meetings over the next few weeks, managers repeated their confession. "No one was prepared to believe us at first," one manager said. "We had screwed up too badly."

At subsequent meetings, management shared with employees the company's dismal business forecast and the limited options available. Without cost reduction, Elco would have to raise its prices, and higher prices would further depress sales. That would mean cutting production even more, perhaps even moving manufacturing offshore. Heads nodded. Employees saw the bind the company was in. The business problem was becoming theirs, not just management's.

But still there were concerns: "If we help to cut costs and learn to produce elevators that are twice as good in half the time, will we work ourselves out of a job?" In response, the managers described their strategy to increase sales outside the United States. They also announced a new policy called *proaction time:* No one would be laid off because of any improvements made by an employee. Instead, employees could use their newly free time to attend cross-training programs designed to give them the skills they would need to work in any area of operations. Or employees could act as consultants addressing quality issues. In addition, management agreed not to replace any departing employees with new hires until business conditions improved. At the same time, however, management made it clear that it retained the right to let people go if business conditions grew worse.

Employees may not have liked what they heard, but they understood it. They began to see that they shared responsibility with management for Elco's success. If they could improve quality and productivity, Elco could bring more value to the market and prevent further sales erosion. To give employees confidence that they were not being misled, management pledged to regularly share data on sales, costs, and market trends—a first step toward rebuilding trust and commitment.

Elco's managers could not undo past mistakes, but they could involve employees in making future decisions. Managers asked employees why they thought the new manufacturing cells weren't working and how to fix them. Employees suggested making changes in the location of materials, in the placement of machines, and in the way tasks were performed. They began to share their knowledge; as they did so, the cells were redesigned and performance steadily improved, often far exceeding the expectations originally set by the consultants. As trust and commitment were restored, talk of bringing the union back died out.

High Park's turn

Meanwhile, management worried about introducing the new work methods at Elco's High Park plant, which, unlike the Chester plant, had a history of resisting change. The union was strong at High Park, and some employees there had as much as 25 years' service. Moreover, the plant manager, a young engineer new to High Park, had never run a plant before. The odds seemed to be against him. If change had created animosity at Chester, one could only imagine how much worse the situation could become at High Park.

But management's fears went unrealized. When the consultants came to the plant, the young manager introduced them to all employees. At a series of plantwide meetings, corporate executives openly discussed business conditions and the company's declining sales and profits. They explained that they had visited other companies' plants and had seen the productivity improvements that cellular manufacturing could bring. They announced the proaction-time policy to calm employees' justifiable fears of layoffs. At the High Park plant, managers encouraged employees to help the consultants design the new manufacturing cells, and they encouraged active debate. Then, as the old performance measures were discarded, managers worked with employees to develop new ones and to establish the cell teams' new responsibilities.

Every day, the High Park plant manager waited for the anticipated meltdown, but it never came. Of course, there were some gripes, but even when people didn't like the decisions, they felt they had been treated fairly and, so, willingly participated in the plant's eventual performance turnaround.

Three years later, we revisited a popular local eatery to talk with people from both plants. Employees from both Chester and High Park now believe that the cellular approach is a better way to work. High Park employees spoke about their plant manager with admiration, and they commiserated with the difficulties Elco's managers had in making the changeover to cellular manufacturing. They concluded that it had been a necessary, worthwhile, and positive experience. But Chester employees spoke with anger and indignation as they described their treatment by Elco's managers. (See "The Price of Unfairness.") For them, as for the London woman who had been unfairly ticketed, fair process was as important as—if not more important than—the outcome.

Fair Process in the Knowledge Economy

Fair process may sound like a soft issue, but understanding its value is crucial for managers trying to adapt their companies to the demands of the knowledge-based economy. Unlike the traditional factors of production—land, labor, and capital—knowledge is a resource locked in the human mind. Creating and sharing knowledge are intangible activities that can neither be supervised nor forced out of people. They happen only when people cooperate voluntarily. As the Nobel laureate economist Friedrich Hayek has argued, "Practically every individual . . . possesses unique information" that can be put to use only with "his active cooperation." Getting that cooperation may well turn out to be one of the key managerial issues of the next few decades. (See "Fair Process Is Critical in Knowledge Work.")

Voluntary cooperation was not what Frederick Winslow Taylor had in mind when at the turn of the century he began to develop an arsenal of tools to promote efficiency and consistency by controlling individuals' behavior and compelling employees to comply with management dictates. Traditional management science, which is rooted in Taylor's time-and-motion studies, encouraged a managerial preoccupation with allocating resources, creating economic incentives and rewards, monitoring and measuring performance, and manipulating organizational structures to set lines of authority. These conventional management levers still have their role to play, but they have little to do with encouraging active cooperation. Instead, they operate in the realm of outcome fairness or what social scientists call *distributive justice,* where the psychology works like this: When people get the compensation (or the resources, or the place in the organizational hierarchy) they deserve, they feel satisfied with that outcome. They will reciprocate by fulfilling to the letter their obligation to the company. The psychology of fair process, or *procedural justice,* is quite different. Fair process builds trust and commitment, trust and commitment produce voluntary cooperation, and voluntary cooperation drives performance, leading people to go beyond the call of duty by sharing their knowledge

KIM AND MAUBORGNE

The Price of Unfairness

Historically, policies designed to establish fair process in organizations arise mainly in reaction to employees' complaints and uprisings. But by then it is too late. When individuals have been so angered by the violation of fair process that they have been driven to organized protest, their demands often stretch well beyond the reasonable to a desire for what theorists call *retributive justice:* Not only do they want fair process restored, they also seek to visit punishment and vengeance upon those who have violated it in compensation for the disrespect the unfair process signals.

Lacking trust in management, employees push for policies that are laboriously detailed, inflexible, and often administratively constricting. They want to ensure that managers will never have the discretion to act unjustly again. In their indignation, they may try to roll back decisions imposed unfairly even when the decisions themselves were good ones—even when they were critical to the company's competitiveness or beneficial to the workers themselves. Such is the emotional power that unfair process can provoke.

Managers who view fair process as a nuisance or as a limit on their freedom to manage must understand that it is the violation of fair process that will wreak the most serious damage on corporate performance. Retribution can be very expensive.

and applying their creativity. In all the management contexts we've studied, whatever the task, we have consistently observed this dynamic at work. (See the exhibit "Two complementary paths to performance.")

Consider the transformation of Bethlehem Steel Corporation's Sparrows Point, Maryland, division, a business unit responsible for marketing, sales, production, and financial performance. Until 1993, the 106-year-old division was managed in the classic command-and-control style. People were expected to do what they were told to do—no more and no less—and management and employees saw themselves as adversaries.

That year, Bethlehem Steel introduced a management model so different at Sparrows Point that Taylor—who was, in fact, the company's consulting engineer about 100 years ago—wouldn't have recognized it. The new model was designed to invoke in employees an active sense of responsibility for sharing their knowledge and ideas with one another and with management. It was also meant to encourage them to take the initiative for getting things done. In the words of Joe Rosel, the president of one of the division's five unions, "It's all about involvement, justification for decisions, and a clear set of expectations."

At Sparrows Point, employees are involved in making and executing decisions at three levels. At the top is a joint-leadership team, composed of senior managers and five employee representatives, that deals with companywide issues when they arise. At the department level are area teams, consisting of managers like superintendents and of employees from the different areas of the plant, such as zone committee people. Those teams deal with day-to-day operational issues such as customer service, quality, and logistics. Ad hoc problem-solving teams of employees address opportunities and obstacles as they arise on the shop floor. At each level, teammates share and debate their ideas. Thus, employees are assured a fair hearing for their points of view on decisions likely to affect them. With the exception of decisions involving major changes or resource commitments, the teams make and execute the decisions themselves.

Sparrows Point uses numerous processes and devices to ensure that all employees can understand why decisions have been made and how such decisions need to be executed. There is, for example, a bulletin board where decisions are posted and explained, allowing employees who haven't been directly involved in those decisions to understand what's going on and why. In addition, in more than 70 four-hour seminars, groups ranging in size from 50 to 250 employees have met to discuss changes occurring at the division, learn about new ideas under consideration, and find out how changes might affect employees' roles and responsibilities. A quarterly newsletter and a monthly "report card" of the division's strategic, marketing, operational, and financial performance keeps each of the unit's 5,300 employees informed. And the teams report back to their colleagues about the changes they are making, seeking help in making the ideas work.

Fair Process Is Critical in Knowledge Work

It is easy to see fair process at work on the plant floor, where its violation can produce such highly visible manifestations as strikes, slowdowns, and high defect rates. But fair process can have an even greater impact on the quality of professional and managerial work. That is because innovation is the key challenge of the knowledge-based economy, and innovation requires the exchange of ideas, which in turn depends on trust.

Executives and professionals rarely walk the picket line, but when their trust has not been won, they frequently withhold their full cooperation—and their ideas. In knowledge work, then, ignoring fair process creates high opportunity costs in the form of ideas that never see daylight and initiatives that are never seized. For example:

A multifunctional team is created to develop an important new product. Because it contains representatives from every major functional area of the company, the team *should* produce more innovative products, with less internal fighting, shortened lead times, and lower costs. The team meets, but people drag their feet. Executives at a computer maker developing a new workstation, for example, thoughtfully deploy the traditional management levers. They hammer out a good incentive scheme. They define the project scope and structure. And they allocate the right resources. Yet the trust, idea sharing, and commitment that everyone wants never materialize. Why? Early in the project, manufacturing and marketing representatives on the team propose building a prototype, but the strong design-engineering group driving the project ignores them. Subsequently, problems surface because the design is difficult to manufacture and the application software is inadequate. The team members from manufacturing and marketing are aware of these issues all along but remain passive in sharing their concerns with the powerful

Fair process has produced significant changes in people's attitudes and behavior. Consider, for example, the tin mill unit at Sparrows Point. In 1992, the unit's performance was among the worst in the industry. But then, as one employee explains, "People started coming forward and sharing their ideas. They started caring about doing great work, not just getting by. Take the success we've had in light-gauge cable sheathing. We had let this high value-added product slip because the long throughput time required for production held up the other mills in the unit. But after we started getting everyone involved and explained why we needed to improve design engineers. Instead, they wait until the problems reveal themselves—at which time they are very expensive to fix.

Two companies create a joint venture that offers clear benefits to both parties. But they then hold their cards so close to their chests that they ensure the alliance will create limited value for either partner. The Chinese joint-venture partner of a European engineering group, for example, withholds critical information from the field, failing to report that customers are having problems installing the partner's products and sitting on requests for new product features. Why do the Chinese fail to cooperate fully, even if it means hurting their own business?

Early in the partnership, the Chinese felt they had been shut out of key product and operating decisions. To make matters worse, the Europeans never explained the logic guiding their decisions. As the Chinese withhold critical information, the increasingly frustrated European partner responds in kind by slowing the transfer of managerial know-how, which the Chinese need badly.

Two companies create a supplier partnership to achieve improved value at lower cost. They agree to act in a seamless fashion, as one company. But the supplier seems to spend more energy on developing other customers than on deepening the partnership. One consumer goods manufacturer, for example, keeps delaying the installation of a joint electronic consumer-response data system with a major food retailer. The system will substantially improve inventory management for both partners. But the supplier remains too wary to invest. Why? The retailer has a history of dropping some of the supplier's products without explanation. And the consumer company can't understand the retailer's ambiguous criteria for designating "preferred suppliers."

throughput, ideas started to flow. At first, the company was doubtful: If the product had created a bottleneck before, why should it be different now? But people came up with the idea of using two sequential mills instead of one to eliminate the bottleneck. Did people suddenly get smarter? No. I'd say they started to care."

The object in creating this new way of working at Sparrows Point was to improve the intellectual buy-in and emotional commitment of employees. It has apparently been successful. Since 1993, Sparrows Point has turned a profit three years in a row, the first time that has happened since the late 1970s. The division is becoming a showcase

Two complementary paths to performance

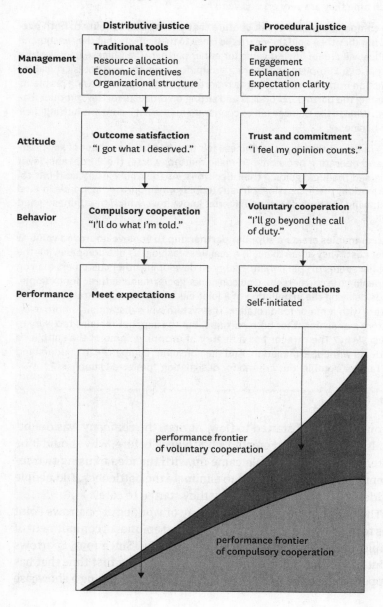

	Distributive justice	Procedural justice
Management tool	**Traditional tools** Resource allocation Economic incentives Organizational structure	**Fair process** Engagement Explanation Expectation clarity
Attitude	**Outcome satisfaction** "I got what I deserved."	**Trust and commitment** "I feel my opinion counts."
Behavior	**Compulsory cooperation** "I'll do what I'm told."	**Voluntary cooperation** "I'll go beyond the call of duty."
Performance	**Meet expectations**	**Exceed expectations** Self-initiated

performance frontier of voluntary cooperation

performance frontier of compulsory cooperation

demonstrating how a declining industry can be revitalized in today's knowledge economy. In the words of one Sparrows Point employee, "Since we know now everything that's going on in the company, we have more trust in management and are more committed to making things happen. People have started doing things beyond the normal call of duty."

Overcoming Mental Barriers

If fair process is such a simple idea and yet so powerful, why do so few companies practice it? Most people think of themselves as fair, and managers are no exception. But if you ask them what it means to be a fair manager, most will describe how they give people the authority they deserve, or the resources they need, or the rewards they have earned. In other words, they will confuse fair process with fair outcomes. The few managers who focus on process might identify only one of the three fair-process principles (the most widely understood is engagement), and they would stop there.

But there are two more fundamental reasons, beyond this simple lack of understanding, that explain why fair process is so rare. The first involves power. Some managers continue to believe that knowledge is power and that they retain power only by keeping what they know to themselves. Their implicit strategy is to preserve their managerial discretion by deliberately leaving the rules for success and failure vague. Other managers maintain control by keeping employees at arm's length, substituting memos and forms for direct, two-way communication, thus avoiding challenges to their ideas or authority. Such styles can reflect deeply ingrained patterns of behavior, and rarely are managers conscious of how they exercise power. For them, fair process would represent a threat.

The second reason is also largely unconscious because it resides in an economic assumption that most of us have grown up taking at face value: the belief that people are concerned only with what's best for themselves. But, as we have seen, there is ample evidence to show that when the process is perceived to be fair, most people will accept outcomes that are not wholly in their favor. People realize that compromises and sacrifices are necessary on the job. They accept the need for short-term personal sacrifices in order to advance the long-term interests of the corporation. Acceptance is conditional, however, hinged as it is on fair process.

Fair process reaches into a dimension of human psychology that hasn't been fully explored in conventional management practice. Yet every company can tap into the voluntary cooperation of its people by building trust through fair processes.

Originally published in July 1997. Reprint R0301K.

Teaching Smart People How to Learn

by Chris Argyris

ANY COMPANY THAT ASPIRES to succeed in the tougher business environment of the 1990s must first resolve a basic dilemma: success in the marketplace increasingly depends on learning, yet most people don't know how to learn. What's more, those members of the organization that many assume to be the best at learning are, in fact, not very good at it. I am talking about the well-educated, high-powered, high-commitment professionals who occupy key leadership positions in the modern corporation.

Most companies not only have tremendous difficulty addressing this learning dilemma; they aren't even aware that it exists. The reason: they misunderstand what learning is and how to bring it about. As a result, they tend to make two mistakes in their efforts to become a learning organization.

First, most people define learning too narrowly as mere "problem solving," so they focus on identifying and correcting errors in the external environment. Solving problems is important. But if learning is to persist, managers and employees must also look inward. They need to reflect critically on their own behavior, identify the ways they often inadvertently contribute to the organization's problems, and then change how they act. In particular, they must learn how the very way they go about defining and solving problems can be a source of problems in its own right.

I have coined the terms "single loop" and "double loop" learning to capture this crucial distinction. To give a simple analogy: a thermostat that automatically turns on the heat whenever the temperature in a room drops below 68 degrees is a good example of single-loop learning. A thermostat that could ask, "Why am I set at 68 degrees?" and then explore whether or not some other temperature might more economically achieve the goal of heating the room would be engaging in double-loop learning.

Highly skilled professionals are frequently very good at single-loop learning. After all, they have spent much of their lives acquiring academic credentials, mastering one or a number of intellectual disciplines, and applying those disciplines to solve real-world problems. But ironically, this very fact helps explain why professionals are often so bad at double-loop learning.

Put simply, because many professionals are almost always successful at what they do, they rarely experience failure. And because they have rarely failed, they have never learned how to learn from failure. So whenever their single-loop learning strategies go wrong, they become defensive, screen out criticism, and put the "blame" on anyone and everyone but themselves. In short, their ability to learn shuts down precisely at the moment they need it the most.

The propensity among professionals to behave defensively helps shed light on the second mistake that companies make about learning. The common assumption is that getting people to learn is largely a matter of motivation. When people have the right attitudes and commitment, learning automatically follows. So companies focus on creating new organizational structures—compensation programs, performance reviews, corporate cultures, and the like—that are designed to create motivated and committed employees.

But effective double-loop learning is not simply a function of how people feel. It is a reflection of how they think—that is, the cognitive rules or reasoning they use to design and implement their actions. Think of these rules as a kind of "master program" stored in the brain, governing all behavior. Defensive reasoning can block learning even when the individual commitment to it is high, just as a

Idea in Brief

Problem solving is an example of **single-loop learning**. You identify an error and apply a particular remedy to correct it. But genuine learning involves an extra step, in which you reflect on your assumptions and test the validity of your hypotheses. Achieving this **double-loop learning** is more than a matter of motivation—you have to reflect on the *way* you think.

Failure forces you to reflect on your assumptions and inferences.

Which is why an organization's smartest and most successful employees are often such poor learners: they haven't had the opportunity for introspection that failure affords. So when they do fail—or merely underperform—they can be surprisingly defensive. Instead of critically examining their own behavior, they cast blame outward—on anyone or anything they can.

computer program with hidden bugs can produce results exactly the opposite of what its designers had planned.

Companies can learn how to resolve the learning dilemma. What it takes is to make the ways managers and employees reason about their behavior a focus of organizational learning and continuous improvement programs. Teaching people how to reason about their behavior in new and more effective ways breaks down the defenses that block learning.

All of the examples that follow involve a particular kind of professional: fast-track consultants at major management consulting companies. But the implications of my argument go far beyond this specific occupational group. The fact is, more and more jobs—no matter what the title—are taking on the contours of "knowledge work." People at all levels of the organization must combine the mastery of some highly specialized technical expertise with the ability to work effectively in teams, form productive relationships with clients and customers, and critically reflect on and then change their own organizational practices. And the nuts and bolts of management—whether of high-powered consultants or service representatives, senior managers or factory technicians—increasingly

Idea in Practice

People often profess to be open to critique and new learning, but their actions suggest a very different set of governing values or theories-in-use:

- the desire to remain in unilateral control
- the goal of maximizing "winning" while minimizing "losing"
- the belief that negative feelings should be suppressed
- the desire to appear as rational as possible.

Taken together, these values betray a profoundly defensive posture: a need to avoid embarrassment, threat, or feelings of vulnerability and incompetence. This **closed-loop reasoning** explains why the mere encouragement of open inquiry can be intimidating to some. And it's especially relevant to the behavior of many of the most highly skilled and best-trained employees. Behind their high aspirations are an equally high fear of failure and a tendency to be ashamed when they don't live up to their high standards. Consequently, they become brittle and despondent in situations in which they don't excel immediately.

Fortunately, it *is* possible for individuals and organizations to develop more productive patterns of behavior. Two suggestions for how to make this happen:

1. **Apply the same kind of "tough reasoning" you use to conduct strategic analysis.** Collect the

consists of guiding and integrating the autonomous but interconnected work of highly skilled people.

How Professionals Avoid Learning

For 15 years, I have been conducting in-depth studies of management consultants. I decided to study consultants for a few simple reasons. First, they are the epitome of the highly educated professionals who play an increasingly central role in all organizations. Almost all of the consultants I've studied have MBAs from the top three or four U.S. business schools. They are also highly committed to their work. For instance, at one company, more than 90% of the consultants responded in a survey that they were "highly satisfied" with their jobs and with the company.

most objective data you can find. Make your inferences explicit and test them constantly. Submit your conclusions to the toughest tests of all: make sure they aren't self-serving or impossible for others to verify.

2. **Senior managers must model the desired changes first.** When the leadership demonstrates its willingness to examine critically its own theories-in-use, changing them as indicated, everyone will find it easier to do the same.

Example: The CEO of an organizational-development firm created a case study to address real problems caused by the intense competition among his direct reports. In a paragraph, he described a meeting he intended to have with his subordinates. Then he wrote down what he planned to say, how he thought his subordinates would respond, as well any thoughts or feelings he thought he might have but not express for fear of derailing the conversation. Instead of actually holding the meeting, he analyzed the scenario he had developed *with* his direct reports. The result was an illuminating conversation in which the CEO and his subordinates were able to circumvent the closed-loop reasoning that had characterized so many prior discussions.

I also assumed that such professional consultants would be good at learning. After all, the essence of their job is to teach others how to do things differently. I found, however, that these consultants embodied the learning dilemma. The most enthusiastic about continuous improvement in their own organizations, they were also often the biggest obstacle to its complete success.

As long as efforts at learning and change focused on external organizational factors—job redesign, compensation programs, performance reviews, and leadership training—the professionals were enthusiastic participants. Indeed, creating new systems and structures was precisely the kind of challenge that well-educated, highly motivated professionals thrived on.

And yet the moment the quest for continuous improvement turned to the professionals' *own* performance, something went wrong. It wasn't a matter of bad attitude. The professionals' commitment to excellence was genuine, and the vision of the company was clear. Nevertheless, continuous improvement did not persist. And the longer the continuous improvement efforts continued, the greater the likelihood that they would produce ever-diminishing returns.

What happened? The professionals began to feel embarrassed. They were threatened by the prospect of critically examining their own role in the organization. Indeed, because they were so well paid (and generally believed that their employers were supportive and fair), the idea that their performance might not be at its best made them feel guilty.

Far from being a catalyst for real change, such feelings caused most to react defensively. They projected the blame for any problems away from themselves and onto what they said were unclear goals, insensitive and unfair leaders, and stupid clients.

Consider this example. At a premier management consulting company, the manager of a case team called a meeting to examine the team's performance on a recent consulting project. The client was largely satisfied and had given the team relatively high marks, but the manager believed the team had not created the value added that it was capable of and that the consulting company had promised. In the spirit of continuous improvement, he felt that the team could do better. Indeed, so did some of the team members.

The manager knew how difficult it was for people to reflect critically on their own work performance, especially in the presence of their manager, so he took a number of steps to make possible a frank and open discussion. He invited to the meeting an outside consultant whom team members knew and trusted—"just to keep me honest," he said. He also agreed to have the entire meeting tape-recorded. That way, any subsequent confusions or disagreements about what went on at the meeting could be checked against the transcript. Finally, the manager opened the meeting by emphasizing that no subject was off limits—including his own behavior.

"I realize that you may believe you cannot confront me," the manager said. "But I encourage you to challenge me. You have a responsibility to tell me where you think the leadership made mistakes, just as I have the responsibility to identify any I believe you made. And all of us must acknowledge our own mistakes. If we do not have an open dialogue, we will not learn."

The professionals took the manager up on the first half of his invitation but quietly ignored the second. When asked to pinpoint the key problems in the experience with the client, they looked entirely outside themselves. The clients were uncooperative and arrogant. "They didn't think we could help them." The team's own managers were unavailable and poorly prepared. "At times, our managers were not up to speed before they walked into the client meetings." In effect, the professionals asserted that they were helpless to act differently—not because of any limitations of their own but because of the limitations of others.

The manager listened carefully to the team members and tried to respond to their criticisms. He talked about the mistakes that he had made during the consulting process. For example, one professional objected to the way the manager had run the project meetings. "I see that the way I asked questions closed down discussions," responded the manager. "I didn't mean to do that, but I can see how you might have believed that I had already made up my mind." Another team member complained that the manager had caved in to pressure from his superior to produce the project report far too quickly, considering the team's heavy work load. "I think that it was my responsibility to have said no," admitted the manager. "It was clear that we all had an immense amount of work."

Finally, after some three hours of discussion about his own behavior, the manager began to ask the team members if there were any errors *they* might have made. "After all," he said, "this client was not different from many others. How can we be more effective in the future?"

The professionals repeated that it was really the clients' and their own managers' fault. As one put it, "They have to be open to change and want to learn." The more the manager tried to get the team to examine its own responsibility for the outcome, the more the professionals bypassed his concerns. The best one team member could suggest was for the case team to "promise less"—implying that there was really no way for the group to improve its performance.

The case team members were reacting defensively to protect themselves, even though their manager was not acting in ways that an outsider would consider threatening. Even if there were some truth to their charges—the clients may well have been arrogant and closed, their own managers distant—the way they presented these claims was guaranteed to stop learning. With few exceptions, the professionals made attributions about the behavior of the clients and the managers but never publicly tested their claims. For instance, they said that the clients weren't motivated to learn but never really presented any evidence supporting that assertion. When their lack of concrete evidence was pointed out to them, they simply repeated their criticisms more vehemently.

If the professionals had felt so strongly about these issues, why had they never mentioned them during the project? According to the professionals, even this was the fault of others. "We didn't want to alienate the client," argued one. "We didn't want to be seen as whining," said another.

The professionals were using their criticisms of others to protect themselves from the potential embarrassment of having to admit that perhaps they too had contributed to the team's less-than-perfect performance. What's more, the fact that they kept repeating their defensive actions in the face of the manager's efforts to turn the group's attention to its own role shows that this defensiveness had become a reflexive routine. From the professionals' perspective, they weren't resisting; they were focusing on the "real" causes. Indeed, they were to be respected, if not congratulated, for working as well as they did under such difficult conditions.

The end result was an unproductive parallel conversation. Both the manager and the professionals were candid; they expressed their views forcefully. But they talked past each other, never finding a common language to describe what had happened with the client. The professionals kept insisting that the fault lay with others. The manager kept trying, unsuccessfully, to get the professionals to see how they contributed to the state of affairs they were criticizing. The dialogue of this parallel conversation looks like this:

Professionals: "The clients have to be open. They must want to change."

Manager: "It's our task to help them see that change is in their interest."

Professionals: "But the clients didn't agree with our analyses."

Manager: "If they didn't think our ideas were right, how might we have convinced them?"

Professionals: "Maybe we need to have more meetings with the client."

Manager: "If we aren't adequately prepared and if the clients don't think we're credible, how will more meetings help?"

Professionals: "There should be better communication between case team members and management."

Manager: "I agree. But professionals should take the initiative to educate the manager about the problems they are experiencing."

Professionals: "Our leaders are unavailable and distant."

Manager: "How do you expect us to know that if you don't tell us?"

Conversations such as this one dramatically illustrate the learning dilemma. The problem with the professionals' claims is not that they are wrong but that they aren't useful. By constantly turning the focus away from their own behavior to that of others, the professionals bring learning to a grinding halt. The manager understands the trap but does not know how to get out of it. To learn how to do that requires going deeper into the dynamics of defensive reasoning—and into the special causes that make professionals so prone to it.

Defensive Reasoning and the Doom Loop

What explains the professionals' defensiveness? Not their attitudes about change or commitment to continuous improvement; they really wanted to work more effectively. Rather, the key factor is the way they reasoned about their behavior and that of others.

It is impossible to reason anew in every situation. If we had to think through all the possible responses every time someone asked, "How are you?" the world would pass us by. Therefore, everyone develops a theory of action—a set of rules that individuals use to design and implement their own behavior as well as to understand the behavior of others. Usually, these theories of actions become so taken for granted that people don't even realize they are using them.

One of the paradoxes of human behavior, however, is that the master program people actually use is rarely the one they think they use. Ask people in an interview or questionnaire to articulate the rules they use to govern their actions, and they will give you what I call their "espoused" theory of action. But observe these same people's behavior, and you will quickly see that this espoused theory has very little to do with how they actually behave. For example, the professionals on the case team said they believed in continuous improvement, and yet they consistently acted in ways that made improvement impossible.

When you observe people's behavior and try to come up with rules that would make sense of it, you discover a very different theory of action—what I call the individual's "theory-in-use." Put simply, people consistently act inconsistently, unaware of the contradiction between their espoused theory and their theory-in-use, between the way they think they are acting and the way they really act.

What's more, most theories-in-use rest on the same set of governing values. There seems to be a universal human tendency to design one's actions consistently according to four basic values:

1. To remain in unilateral control;

2. To maximize "winning" and minimize "losing";

3. To suppress negative feelings; and

4. To be as "rational" as possible—by which people mean defining clear objectives and evaluating their behavior in terms of whether or not they have achieved them.

The purpose of all these values is to avoid embarrassment or threat, feeling vulnerable or incompetent. In this respect, the master program that most people use is profoundly defensive. Defensive reasoning encourages individuals to keep private the premises, inferences, and conclusions that shape their behavior and to avoid testing them in a truly independent, objective fashion.

Because the attributions that go into defensive reasoning are never really tested, it is a closed loop, remarkably impervious to conflicting points of view. The inevitable response to the observation that somebody is reasoning defensively is yet more defensive reasoning. With the case team, for example, whenever anyone pointed out the professionals' defensive behavior to them, their initial reaction was to look for the cause in somebody else—clients who were so sensitive that they would have been alienated if the consultants had criticized them or a manager so weak that he couldn't have taken it had the consultants raised their concerns with him. In other words, the case team members once again denied their own responsibility by externalizing the problem and putting it on someone else.

In such situations, the simple act of encouraging more open inquiry is often attacked by others as "intimidating." Those who do the attacking deal with their feelings about possibly being wrong by blaming the more open individual for arousing these feelings and upsetting them.

Needless to say, such a master program inevitably short-circuits learning. And for a number of reasons unique to their psychology, well-educated professionals are especially susceptible to this.

Nearly all the consultants I have studied have stellar academic records. Ironically, their very success at education helps explain the problems they have with learning. Before they enter the world of work, their lives are primarily full of successes, so they have rarely experienced the embarrassment and sense of threat that comes with failure. As a result, their defensive reasoning has rarely been activated. People who rarely experience failure, however, end up not knowing how to deal with it effectively. And this serves to reinforce the normal human tendency to reason defensively.

In a survey of several hundred young consultants at the organizations I have been studying, these professionals describe themselves as driven internally by an unrealistically high ideal of performance: "Pressure on the job is self-imposed." "I must not only do a good job; I must also be the best." "People around here are very bright and hardworking; they are highly motivated to do an outstanding job." "Most of us want not only to succeed but also to do so at maximum speed."

These consultants are always comparing themselves with the best around them and constantly trying to better their own performance. And yet they do not appreciate being required to compete openly with each other. They feel it is somehow inhumane. They prefer to be the individual contributor—what might be termed a "productive loner."

Behind this high aspiration for success is an equally high fear of failure and a propensity to feel shame and guilt when they do fail to meet their high standards. "You must avoid mistakes," said one. "I hate making them. Many of us fear failure, whether we admit it or not."

To the extent that these consultants have experienced success in their lives, they have not had to be concerned about failure and the attendant feelings of shame and guilt. But to exactly the same extent, they also have never developed the tolerance for feelings of failure or the skills to deal with these feelings. This in turn has led them not only to fear failure but also to fear the fear of failure itself. For they know that they will not cope with it superlatively—their usual level of aspiration.

The consultants use two intriguing metaphors to describe this phenomenon. They talk about the "doom loop" and "doom zoom." Often, consultants will perform well on the case team, but because they don't do the jobs perfectly or receive accolades from their managers, they go into a doom loop of despair. And they don't ease into the doom loop, they zoom into it.

As a result, many professionals have extremely "brittle" personalities. When suddenly faced with a situation they cannot immediately handle, they tend to fall apart. They cover up their distress in front of the client. They talk about it constantly with their fellow case team members. Interestingly, these conversations commonly take the form of bad-mouthing clients.

Such brittleness leads to an inappropriately high sense of despondency or even despair when people don't achieve the high levels of performance they aspire to. Such despondency is rarely psychologically devastating, but when combined with defensive reasoning, it can result in a formidable predisposition against learning.

There is no better example of how this brittleness can disrupt an organization than performance evaluations. Because it represents the one moment when a professional must measure his or her own behavior against some formal standard, a performance evaluation is almost tailor-made to push a professional into the doom loop. Indeed, a poor evaluation can reverberate far beyond the particular individual involved to spark defensive reasoning throughout an entire organization.

At one consulting company, management established a new performance-evaluation process that was designed to make evaluations both more objective and more useful to those being evaluated. The consultants participated in the design of the new system and in general were enthusiastic because it corresponded to their espoused values of objectivity and fairness. A brief two years into the new process, however, it had become the object of dissatisfaction. The catalyst for this about-face was the first unsatisfactory rating.

Senior managers had identified six consultants whose performance they considered below standard. In keeping with the new evaluation process, they did all they could to communicate their concerns to the six and to help them improve. Managers met with each individual separately for as long and as often as the professional requested to explain the reasons behind the rating and to discuss what needed to be done to improve—but to no avail. Performance continued at the same low level and, eventually, the six were let go.

When word of the dismissal spread through the company, people responded with confusion and anxiety. After about a dozen consultants angrily complained to management, the CEO held two lengthy meetings where employees could air their concerns.

At the meetings, the professionals made a variety of claims. Some said the performance-evaluation process was unfair because judgments were subjective and biased and the criteria for minimum performance unclear. Others suspected that the real cause for the dismissals was economic and that the performance-evaluation procedure was just a fig leaf to hide the fact that the company was in trouble. Still others argued that the evaluation process was antilearning. If the company were truly a learning organization, as it claimed, then people performing below the minimum standard should be taught how to reach it. As one professional put it: "We were told that the company did not have an up-or-out policy. Up-or-out is inconsistent with learning. You misled us."

The CEO tried to explain the logic behind management's decision by grounding it in the facts of the case and by asking the professionals for any evidence that might contradict these facts.

Is there subjectivity and bias in the evaluation process? Yes, responded the CEO, but "we strive hard to reduce them. We are constantly trying to improve the process. If you have any ideas, please tell us. If you know of someone treated unfairly, please bring it up. If any of you feel that you have been treated unfairly, let's discuss it now or, if you wish, privately."

Is the level of minimum competence too vague? "We are working to define minimum competence more clearly," he answered. "In the case of the six, however, their performance was so poor that it wasn't difficult to reach a decision." Most of the six had received timely feedback about their problems. And in the two cases where people had not, the reason was that they had never taken the responsibility to seek out evaluations—and, indeed, had actively avoided them. "If you have any data to the contrary," the CEO added, "let's talk about it."

Were the six asked to leave for economic reasons? No, said the CEO. "We have more work than we can do, and letting professionals go is extremely costly for us. Do any of you have any information to the contrary?"

As to the company being antilearning, in fact, the entire evaluation process was designed to encourage learning. When a professional is performing below the minimum level, the CEO explained, "we jointly design remedial experiences with the individual. Then we look for signs of improvement. In these cases, either the professionals were reluctant to take on such assignments or they repeatedly failed when they did. Again, if you have information or evidence to the contrary, I'd like to hear about it."

The CEO concluded: "It's regrettable, but sometimes we make mistakes and hire the wrong people. If individuals don't produce and repeatedly prove themselves unable to improve, we don't know what else to do except dismiss them. It's just not fair to keep poorly performing individuals in the company. They earn an unfair share of the financial rewards."

Instead of responding with data of their own, the professionals simply repeated their accusations but in ways that consistently contradicted their claims. They said that a genuinely fair evaluation process would contain clear and documentable data about performance—but they were unable to provide firsthand examples of the unfairness that they implied colored the evaluation of the six dismissed employees. They argued that people shouldn't be judged by inferences unconnected to their actual performance—but they judged management in precisely this way. They insisted that management define clear, objective, and unambiguous performance standards—but they argued that any humane system would take into account that the performance of a professional cannot be precisely measured. Finally, they presented themselves as champions of learning—but they never proposed any criteria for assessing whether an individual might be unable to learn.

In short, the professionals seemed to hold management to a different level of performance than they held themselves. In their conversation at the meetings, they used many of the features of ineffective evaluation that they condemned—the absence of concrete data, for example, and the dependence on a circular logic of "heads we win, tails you lose." It is as if they were saying, "Here are the features of a fair performance-evaluation system. You should abide by them. But we don't have to when we are evaluating you."

Indeed, if we were to explain the professionals' behavior by articulating rules that would have to be in their heads in order for them to act the way they did, the rules would look something like this:

1. When criticizing the company, state your criticism in ways that you believe are valid—but also in ways that prevent others from deciding for themselves whether your claim to validity is correct.

2. When asked to illustrate your criticisms, don't include any data that others could use to decide for themselves whether the illustrations are valid.

3. State your conclusions in ways that disguise their logical implications. If others point out those implications to you, deny them.

Of course, when such rules were described to the professionals, they found them abhorrent. It was inconceivable that these rules might explain their actions. And yet in defending themselves against this observation, they almost always inadvertently confirmed the rules.

Learning How to Reason Productively

If defensive reasoning is as widespread as I believe, then focusing on an individual's attitudes or commitment is never enough to produce real change. And as the previous example illustrates, neither is creating new organizational structures or systems. The problem is that even when people are genuinely committed to improving their performance and management has changed its structures in order to encourage the "right" kind of behavior, people still remain locked in defensive reasoning. Either they remain unaware of this fact, or if they do become aware of it, they blame others.

There is, however, reason to believe that organizations can break out of this vicious circle. Despite the strength of defensive reasoning, people genuinely strive to produce what they intend. They value acting competently. Their self-esteem is intimately tied up with behaving consistently and performing effectively. Companies can use these universal human tendencies to teach people how to reason in a new way—in effect, to change the master programs in their heads and thus reshape their behavior.

People can be taught how to recognize the reasoning they use when they design and implement their actions. They can begin to identify the inconsistencies between their espoused and actual theories of action. They can face up to the fact that they unconsciously design and implement actions that they do not intend. Finally, people can learn how to identify what individuals and groups do to create organizational defenses and how these defenses contribute to an organization's problems.

Once companies embark on this learning process, they will discover that the kind of reasoning necessary to reduce and overcome organizational defenses is the same kind of "tough reasoning" that underlies the effective use of ideas in strategy, finance, marketing, manufacturing, and other management disciplines. Any sophisticated strategic analysis, for example, depends on collecting valid data, analyzing it carefully, and constantly testing the inferences drawn from the data. The toughest tests are reserved for the conclusions. Good strategists make sure that their conclusions can withstand all kinds of critical questioning.

So too with productive reasoning about human behavior. The standard of analysis is just as high. Human resource programs no longer need to be based on "soft" reasoning but should be as analytical and as data-driven as any other management discipline.

Of course, that is not the kind of reasoning the consultants used when they encountered problems that were embarrassing or threatening. The data they collected was hardly objective. The inferences they made rarely became explicit. The conclusions they reached were largely self-serving, impossible for others to test, and as a result, "self-sealing," impervious to change.

How can an organization begin to turn this situation around, to teach its members how to reason productively? The first step is for managers at the top to examine critically and change their own theories-in-use. Until senior managers become aware of how they reason defensively and the counterproductive consequences that result, there will be little real progress. Any change activity is likely to be just a fad.

Change has to start at the top because otherwise defensive senior managers are likely to disown any transformation in reasoning patterns coming from below. If professionals or middle managers begin to change the way they reason and act, such changes are likely to appear strange—if not actually dangerous—to those at the top. The result is an unstable situation where senior managers still believe that it is a sign of caring and sensitivity to bypass and cover up difficult issues, while their subordinates see the very same actions as defensive.

The key to any educational experience designed to teach senior managers how to reason productively is to connect the program to real business problems. The best demonstration of the usefulness of productive reasoning is for busy managers to see how it can make a direct difference in their own performance and in that of the organization. This will not happen overnight. Managers need plenty of opportunity to practice the new skills. But once they grasp the powerful impact that productive reasoning can have on actual performance, they will have a strong incentive to reason productively not just in a training session but in all their work relationships.

One simple approach I have used to get this process started is to have participants produce a kind of rudimentary case study. The subject is a real business problem that the manager either wants to deal with or has tried unsuccessfully to address in the past. Writing the actual case usually takes less than an hour. But then the case becomes the focal point of an extended analysis.

For example, a CEO at a large organizational-development consulting company was preoccupied with the problems caused by the intense competition among the various business functions represented by his four direct reports. Not only was he tired of having the problems dumped in his lap, but he was also worried about the impact the interfunctional conflicts were having on the organization's flexibility. He had even calculated that the money being spent to iron out disagreements amounted to hundreds of thousands of dollars every year. And the more fights there were, the more defensive people became, which only increased the costs to the organization.

In a paragraph or so, the CEO described a meeting he intended to have with his direct reports to address the problem. Next, he divided the paper in half, and on the right-hand side of the page, he wrote a scenario for the meeting—much like the script for a movie or play—describing what he would say and how his subordinates would likely respond. On the left-hand side of the page, he wrote down any thoughts and feelings that he would be likely to have during the meeting but that he wouldn't express for fear they would derail the discussion.

But instead of holding the meeting, the CEO analyzed this scenario *with* his direct reports. The case became the catalyst for a discussion in which the CEO learned several things about the way he acted with his management team.

He discovered that his four direct reports often perceived his conversations as counterproductive. In the guise of being "diplomatic," he would pretend that a consensus about the problem existed, when in fact none existed. The unintended result: instead of feeling reassured, his subordinates felt wary and tried to figure out "what is he *really* getting at."

The CEO also realized that the way he dealt with the competitiveness among department heads was completely contradictory. On the one hand, he kept urging them to "think of the organization as a whole." On the other, he kept calling for actions—department budget cuts, for example—that placed them directly in competition with each other.

Finally, the CEO discovered that many of the tacit evaluations and attributions he had listed turned out to be wrong. Since he had never expressed these assumptions, he had never found out just how wrong they were. What's more, he learned that much of what he thought he was hiding came through to his subordinates anyway—but with the added message that the boss was covering up.

The CEO's colleagues also learned about their own ineffective behavior. They learned by examining their own behavior as they tried to help the CEO analyze his case. They also learned by writing and analyzing cases of their own. They began to see that they too tended to bypass and cover up the real issues and that the CEO was often aware of it but did not say so. They too made inaccurate attributions and evaluations that they did not express. Moreover, the belief that they had to hide important ideas and feelings from the CEO and from each other in order not to upset anyone turned out to be mistaken. In the context of the case discussions, the entire senior management team was quite willing to discuss what had always been undiscussable.

In effect, the case study exercise legitimizes talking about issues that people have never been able to address before. Such a discussion can be emotional—even painful. But for managers with the courage to persist, the payoff is great: management teams and entire organizations work more openly and more effectively and have greater options for behaving flexibly and adapting to particular situations.

When senior managers are trained in new reasoning skills, they can have a big impact on the performance of the entire organization— even when other employees are still reasoning defensively. The CEO who led the meetings on the performance-evaluation procedure was able to defuse dissatisfaction because he didn't respond to professionals' criticisms in kind but instead gave a clear presentation of relevant data. Indeed, most participants took the CEO's behavior to be a sign that the company really acted on the values of participation and employee involvement that it espoused.

Of course, the ideal is for all the members of an organization to learn how to reason productively. This has happened at the company where the case team meeting took place. Consultants and their managers are now able to confront some of the most difficult issues of the consultant-client relationship. To get a sense of the difference productive reasoning can make, imagine how the original conversation between the manager and case team might have gone had everyone engaged in effective reasoning. (The following dialogue is based on actual sessions I have attended with other case teams at the same company since the training has been completed.)

First, the consultants would have demonstrated their commitment to continuous improvement by being willing to examine their own role in the difficulties that arose during the consulting project. No doubt they would have identified their managers and the clients as part of the problem, but they would have gone on to admit that they had contributed to it as well. More important, they would have agreed with the manager that as they explored the various roles of clients, managers, and professionals, they would make sure to test any evaluations or attributions they might make against the data. Each individual would have encouraged the others to question his or her reasoning. Indeed, they would have insisted on it. And in turn, everyone would have understood that act of questioning not as a sign of mistrust or an invasion of privacy but as a valuable opportunity for learning.

The conversation about the manager's unwillingness to say no might look something like this:

Professional #1: "One of the biggest problems I had with the way you managed this case was that you seemed to be unable to say no when either the client or your superior made unfair demands." [Gives an example.]

Professional #2: "I have another example to add. [Describes a second example.] But I'd also like to say that we never really told you how we felt about this. Behind your back we were bad-mouthing you—you know, 'he's being such a wimp'—but we never came right out and said it."

Manager: "It certainly would have been helpful if you had said something. Was there anything I said or did that gave you the idea that you had better not raise this with me?"

Professional #3: "Not really. I think we didn't want to sound like we were whining."

Manager: "Well, I certainly don't think you sound like you're whining. But two thoughts come to mind. If I understand you correctly, you *were* complaining, but the complaining about me and my inability to say no was covered up. Second, if we had discussed this, I might have gotten the data I needed to be able to say no."

Notice that when the second professional describes how the consultants had covered up their complaints, the manager doesn't criticize her. Rather, he rewards her for being open by responding in kind. He focuses on the ways that he too may have contributed to the cover-up. Reflecting undefensively about his own role in the problem then makes it possible for the professionals to talk about their fears of appearing to be whining. The manager then agrees with the professionals that they shouldn't become complainers. At the same time, he points out the counterproductive consequences of covering up their complaints.

Another unresolved issue in the case team meeting concerned the supposed arrogance of the clients. A more productive conversation about that problem might go like this:

Manager: "You said that the clients were arrogant and uncooperative. What did they say and do?"

Professional #1: "One asked me if I had ever met a payroll. Another asked how long I've been out of school."

Professional #2: "One even asked me how old I was!"

Professional #3: "That's nothing. The worst is when they say that all we do is interview people, write a report based on what they tell us, and then collect our fees."

Manager: "The fact that we tend to be so young is a real problem for many of our clients. They get very defensive about it. But I'd like to explore whether there is a way for them to freely express their views without our getting defensive..."

"What troubled me about your original responses was that you assumed you were right in calling the clients stupid. One thing I've noticed about consultants—in this company and others—is that we tend to defend ourselves by bad-mouthing the client."

Professional #1: "Right. After all, if they are genuinely stupid, then it's obviously not our fault that they aren't getting it!"

Professional #2: "Of course, that stance is antilearning and over-protective. By assuming that they can't learn, we absolve ourselves from having to."

Professional #3: "And the more we all go along with the bad-mouthing, the more we reinforce each other's defensiveness."

Manager: "So what's the alternative? How can we encourage our clients to express their defensiveness and at the same time constructively build on it?"

Professional #1: "We all know that the real issue isn't our age; it's whether or not we are able to add value to the client's organization. They should judge us by what we produce. And if we aren't adding value, they should get rid of us—no matter how young or old we happen to be."

Manager: "Perhaps that is exactly what we should tell them."

In both these examples, the consultants and their manager are doing real work. They are learning about their own group dynamics and addressing some generic problems in client-consultant relationships. The insights they gain will allow them to act more effectively in the future—both as individuals and as a team. They are not just solving problems but developing a far deeper and more textured understanding of their role as members of the organization. They are laying the groundwork for continuous improvement that is truly continuous. They are learning how to learn.

Originally published in May 1991. Reprint 4304.

155

How (Un)ethical Are You?

by Mahzarin R. Banaji, Max H. Bazerman, and Dolly Chugh

ANSWER TRUE OR FALSE: "I am an ethical manager."

If you answered "true," here's an uncomfortable fact: You're probably not. Most of us believe that we are ethical and unbiased. We imagine we're good decision makers, able to objectively size up a job candidate or a venture deal and reach a fair and rational conclusion that's in our, and our organization's, best interests. But more than two decades of research confirms that, in reality, most of us fall woefully short of our inflated self-perception. We're deluded by what Yale psychologist David Armor calls the illusion of objectivity, the notion that we're free of the very biases we're so quick to recognize in others. What's more, these unconscious, or implicit, biases can be contrary to our consciously held, explicit beliefs. We may believe with confidence and conviction that a job candidate's race has no bearing on our hiring decisions or that we're immune to conflicts of interest. But psychological research routinely exposes counterintentional, unconscious biases. The prevalence of these biases suggests that even the most well-meaning person unwittingly allows unconscious thoughts and feelings to influence seemingly objective decisions. These flawed judgments are ethically problematic and undermine managers' fundamental work—to recruit and retain superior talent, boost the performance of individuals and teams, and collaborate effectively with partners.

This article explores four related sources of unintentional unethical decision making: implicit forms of prejudice, bias that favors one's own group, conflict of interest, and a tendency to overclaim credit. Because we are not consciously aware of these sources of bias, they often cannot be addressed by penalizing people for their bad decisions. Nor are they likely to be corrected through conventional ethics training. Rather, managers must bring a new type of vigilance to bear. To begin, this requires letting go of the notion that our conscious attitudes always represent what we think they do. It also demands that we abandon our faith in our own objectivity and our ability to be fair. In the following pages, we will offer strategies that can help managers recognize these pervasive, corrosive, unconscious biases and reduce their impact.

Implicit Prejudice: Bias That Emerges from Unconscious Beliefs

Most fair-minded people strive to judge others according to their merits, but our research shows how often people instead judge according to unconscious stereotypes and attitudes, or "implicit prejudice." What makes implicit prejudice so common and persistent is that it is rooted in the fundamental mechanics of thought. Early on, we learn to associate things that commonly go together and expect them to inevitably coexist: thunder and rain, for instance, or gray hair and old age. This skill—to perceive and learn from associations—often serves us well.

But, of course, our associations only reflect approximations of the truth; they are rarely applicable to every encounter. Rain doesn't always accompany thunder, and the young can also go gray. Nonetheless, because we automatically make such associations to help us organize our world, we grow to trust them, and they can blind us to those instances in which the associations are not accurate—when they don't align with our expectations.

Because implicit prejudice arises from the ordinary and unconscious tendency to make associations, it is distinct from conscious forms of prejudice, such as overt racism or sexism. This distinction

Idea in Brief

Are you an ethical manager? Most would probably say, "Of course!" The truth is, most of us are not.

Most of us believe that we're ethical and unbiased. We assume that we objectively size up job candidates or venture deals and reach fair and rational conclusions that are in our organization's best interests.

But the truth is, we harbor many unconscious—and unethical—biases that derail our decisions and undermine our work as managers. Hidden biases prevent us from recognizing high-potential workers and retaining talented managers. They stop us from collaborating effectively with partners. They erode our teams' performance.

They can also lead to costly lawsuits.

But how can we root out these biases if they're unconscious? Fortunately, as a manager, you can take deliberate actions to counteract their pull. **Regularly audit your decisions.** Have you, for example, hired a disproportionate number of people of your own race? **Expose yourself to non-stereotypical environments** that challenge your biases. If your department is led by men, spend time in one with women in leadership positions. And **consider counterintuitive options** when making decisions. Don't rely on a mental short-list of candidates for a new assignment; consider every employee with relevant qualifications.

explains why people who are free from conscious prejudice may still harbor biases and act accordingly. Exposed to images that juxtapose black men and violence, portray women as sex objects, imply that the physically disabled are mentally weak and the poor are lazy, even the most consciously unbiased person is bound to make biased associations. These associations play out in the workplace just as they do anywhere else.

In the mid-1990s, Tony Greenwald, a professor of psychology at the University of Washington, developed an experimental tool called the Implicit Association Test (IAT) to study unconscious bias. A computerized version of the test requires subjects to rapidly classify words and images as "good" or "bad." Using a keyboard, test takers must make split-second "good/bad" distinctions between words like "love," "joy," "pain," and "sorrow" and at the same time sort images of faces that are (depending on the bias in question) black or white,

Idea in Practice

Unconscious Biases

Are the following unconscious biases levying what amounts to a "stereotype tax" on your company?

Implicit prejudice Judging according to unconscious stereotypes rather than merit exacts a high business cost. Exposed to images that juxtapose physical disabilities with mental weakness or portray poor people as lazy, even the most consciously unbiased person is bound to make biased associations. As a result, we routinely overlook highly qualified candidates for assignments.

In-group favoritism Granting favors to people with your same background—your nationality or alma mater—effectively discriminates against those who are different from you. Consider the potential cost of offering bonuses to employees who refer their friends for job openings: hires who may not have made the grade *without* in-group favoritism.

Overclaiming credit Most of us consider ourselves above average. But when every member of a team thinks he's making the biggest contribution, each starts to think the others aren't pulling their weight. That jeopardizes future collaborations. It also frustrates talented workers who may resign because they feel underappreciated.

young or old, fat or thin, and so on. The test exposes implicit biases by detecting subtle shifts in reaction time that can occur when test takers are required to pair different sets of words and faces. Subjects who consciously believe that they have no negative feelings toward, say, black Americans or the elderly are nevertheless likely to be slower to associate elderly or black faces with the "good" words than they are to associate youthful or white faces with "good" words.

Since 1998, when Greenwald, Brian Nosek, and Mahzarin Banaji put the IAT online, people from around the world have taken over 2.5 million tests, confirming and extending the findings of more traditional laboratory experiments. Both show implicit biases to be strong and pervasive. (For more information on the IAT, see "Are You Biased?".)

Counteract Biases

To keep yourself from making similarly skewed calls, consider these guidelines:

Gather better data Expose your own implicit biases. Take the Implicit Association Test (at http://implicit.harvard.edu). If you discover gender or racial biases, examine your hiring and promotion decisions in that new light. When working with others, have team members estimate their colleagues' contributions *before* they claim their own credit.

Rid your workplace of stereotypical cues Think about the biased associations your workplace may foster. Do your company's advertising and marketing materials frequently include sports metaphors or high-tech jargon? Make a conscious effort to curb such "insider" language—making your products more appealing to a diverse customer base. And if your department invariably promotes the same type of manager—highly analytic, for instance—shadow a department that values a different—perhaps more conceptual—skill-set.

Broaden your mind-set when making decisions Apply the "veil of ignorance" to your next managerial decision. Suppose you're considering a new policy that would give more vacation time to all employees but eliminate the flextime that has allowed new parents to keep working. How would your opinion differ if you were a parent or childless? Male or female? Healthy or unhealthy? You'll learn how strongly implicit biases influence you.

Biases are also likely to be costly. In controlled experiments, psychologists Laurie Rudman at Rutgers and Peter Glick at Lawrence University have studied how implicit biases may work to exclude qualified people from certain roles. One set of experiments examined the relationship between participants' implicit gender stereotypes and their hiring decisions. Those holding stronger implicit biases were less likely to select a qualified woman who exhibited stereotypically "masculine" personality qualities, such as ambition or independence, for a job requiring stereotypically "feminine" qualities, such as interpersonal skills. Yet they would select a qualified man exhibiting these same qualities. The hirers' biased perception was that the woman was less likely to be socially skilled than the man, though their qualifications were in fact the same. These results suggest that implicit biases may exact costs by subtly excluding qualified people from the very organizations that seek their talents.

Legal cases also reveal the real costs of implicit biases, both economic and social. Consider *Price Waterhouse v. Hopkins*. Despite logging more billable hours than her peers, bringing in $25 million to the company, and earning the praise of her clients, Ann Hopkins was turned down for partner, and she sued. The details of the case reveal that her evaluators were explicitly prejudiced in their attitudes. For example, they had commented that Ann "overcompensated for being a woman" and needed a "course at charm school." But perhaps more damning from a legal standpoint was blunt testimony from experimental research. Testifying as an expert witness for the defense, psychology professor Susan Fiske, now at Princeton University, argued that the potential for biased decision making is *inherent* in a system in which a person has "solo" status—that is, a system in which the person is the only one of a kind (the only woman, the only African-American, the only person with a disability, and the like). Judge Gerhard Gesell concluded that "a far more subtle process [than the usual discriminatory intent] is involved" in the assessments made of Ann Hopkins, and she won both in a lower court and in the Supreme Court in what is now a landmark case in discrimination law.

Likewise, the 1999 case of *Thomas v. Kodak* demonstrates that implicit biases can be the basis for rulings. Here, the court posed the question of "whether the employer consciously intended to base the evaluations on race or simply did so because of unthinking stereotypes or bias." The court concluded that plaintiffs can indeed challenge "subjective evaluations which could easily mask covert or unconscious race discrimination." Although courts are careful not to assign responsibility easily for unintentional biases, these cases demonstrate the potential for corporate liability that such patterns of behavior could unwittingly create.

In-Group Favoritism: Bias That Favors Your Group

Think about some of the favors you have done in recent years, whether for a friend, a relative, or a colleague. Have you helped someone get a useful introduction, admission to a school, or a job? Most of us are glad to help out with such favors. Not surprisingly, we tend to do more favors for those we know, and those we know tend to be like ourselves: people who share our nationality, social class, and perhaps religion, race, employer, or alma mater. This all sounds rather innocent. What's wrong with asking your neighbor, the university dean, to meet with a coworker's son? Isn't it just being helpful to recommend a former sorority sister for a job or to talk to your banker cousin when a friend from church gets turned down for a home loan?

Few people set out to exclude anyone through such acts of kindness. But when those in the majority or those in power allocate scarce resources (such as jobs, promotions, and mortgages) to people just like them, they effectively discriminate against those who are different from them. Such "in-group favoritism" amounts to giving extra credit for group membership. Yet while discriminating against those who are different is considered unethical, helping people close to us is often viewed favorably. Think about the number of companies that explicitly encourage this by offering hiring bonuses to employees who refer their friends for job opportunities.

But consider the finding that banks in the United States are more likely to deny a mortgage application from a black person than from a white person, even when the applicants are equally qualified. The common view has been that banks are hostile to African-Americans. While this may be true of some banks and some loan officers, social psychologist David Messick has argued that in-group favoritism is more likely to be at the root of such discriminatory lending. A white loan officer may feel hopeful or lenient toward an unqualified white applicant while following the bank's lending standards strictly with an unqualified black applicant. In denying the black applicant's mortgage, the loan officer may not be expressing hostility toward blacks so much as favoritism toward whites. It's a subtle but crucial distinction.

The ethical cost is clear and should be reason enough to address the problem. But such inadvertent bias produces an additional effect: It erodes the bottom line. Lenders who discriminate in this way,

Are You Biased?

ARE YOU WILLING TO bet that you feel the same way toward European-Americans as you do toward African-Americans? How about women versus men? Or older people versus younger ones? Think twice before you take that bet. Visit implicit.harvard.edu or www.tolerance.org/hidden_bias to examine your unconscious attitudes.

The Implicit Association Tests available on these sites reveal unconscious beliefs by asking takers to make split-second associations between words with positive or negative connotations and images representing different types of people. The various tests on these sites expose the differences—or the alignment—between test takers' conscious and unconscious attitudes toward people of different races, sexual orientation, or physical characteristics. Data gathered from over 2.5 million online tests and further research tells us that unconscious biases are:

- **widely prevalent.** At least 75% of test takers show an implicit bias favoring the young, the rich, and whites.

- **robust.** The mere conscious desire not to be biased does not eliminate implicit bias.

- **contrary to conscious intention.** Although people tend to report little or no *conscious* bias against African-Americans, Arabs, Arab-Americans, Jews, gay men, lesbians, or the poor, they show substantial biases on implicit measures.

- **different in degree depending on group status.** Minority group members tend to show less implicit preference for their own group than majority group members show for theirs. For example, African-Americans report strong preference for their group on explicit measures but show relatively less implicit preference in the tests. Conversely, white Americans report a low explicit bias for their group but a higher implicit bias.

- **consequential.** Those who show higher levels of bias on the IAT are also likely to behave in ways that are more biased in face-to-face interactions with members of the group they are biased against and in the choices they make, such as hiring decisions.

- **costly.** Research currently under way in our lab suggests that implicit bias generates a "stereotype tax"—negotiators leave money on the table because biases cause them to miss opportunities to learn about their opponent and thus create additional value through mutually beneficial trade-offs.

for example, incur bad-debt costs they could have avoided if their lending decisions were more objective. They also may find themselves exposed to damaging publicity or discrimination lawsuits if the skewed lending pattern is publicly revealed. In a different context, companies may pay a real cost for marginal hires who wouldn't have made the grade but for the sympathetic hiring manager swayed by in-group favoritism.

In-group favoritism is tenacious when membership confers clear advantages, as it does, for instance, among whites and other dominant social groups. (It may be weaker or absent among people whose group membership offers little societal advantage.) Thus for a wide array of managerial tasks—from hiring, firing, and promoting to contracting services and forming partnerships—qualified minority candidates are subtly and unconsciously discriminated against, sometimes simply because they are in the minority: There are not enough of them to counter the propensity for in-group favoritism in the majority.

Overclaiming Credit: Bias That Favors You

It's only natural for successful people to hold positive views about themselves. But many studies show that the majority of people consider themselves above average on a host of measures, from intelligence to driving ability. Business executives are no exception. We tend to overrate our individual contribution to groups, which, bluntly put, tends to lead to an overblown sense of entitlement. We become the unabashed, repeated beneficiaries of this unconscious bias, and the more we think only of our own contributions, the less fairly we judge others with whom we work.

Lab research demonstrates this most personal of biases. At Harvard, Eugene Caruso, Nick Epley, and Max Bazerman recently asked MBA students in study groups to estimate what portion of their group's work each had done. The sum of the contribution by all members, of course, must add up to 100%. But the researchers found that the totals for each study group averaged 139%. In a related study, Caruso and his colleagues uncovered rampant overestimates by academic authors of their contribution to shared research projects. Sadly, but not surprisingly, the more the sum of the total estimated group effort exceeded 100% (in other words, the more credit each person claimed), the less the parties wanted to collaborate in the future.

Likewise in business, claiming too much credit can destabilize alliances. When each party in a strategic partnership claims too much credit for its own contribution and becomes skeptical about whether the other is doing its fair share, they both tend to reduce their contributions to compensate. This has obvious repercussions for the joint venture's performance.

Unconscious overclaiming can be expected to reduce the performance and longevity of groups within organizations, just as it diminished the academic authors' willingness to collaborate. It can also take a toll on employee commitment. Think about how employees perceive raises. Most are not so different from the children at Lake Wobegon, believing that they, too, rank in the upper half of their peer group. But many necessarily get pay increases that are below the average. If an employee learns of a colleague's greater compensation—while honestly believing that he himself is more deserving—resentment may be natural. At best, his resentment might translate into reduced commitment and performance. At worst, he may leave the organization that, it seems, doesn't appreciate his contribution.

Conflict of Interest: Bias That Favors Those Who Can Benefit You

Everyone knows that conflict of interest can lead to intentionally corrupt behavior. But numerous psychological experiments show how powerfully such conflicts can unintentionally skew decision making. (For an examination of the evidence in one business arena, see Max Bazerman, George Loewenstein, and Don Moore's November 2002 HBR article, "Why Good Accountants Do Bad Audits.") These experiments suggest that the work world is rife with situations in which such conflicts lead honest, ethical professionals to unconsciously make unsound and unethical recommendations.

Physicians, for instance, face conflicts of interest when they accept payment for referring patients into clinical trials. While, surely, most physicians consciously believe that their referrals are the patient's best clinical option, how do they know that the promise of payment did not skew their decisions? Similarly, many lawyers earn fees based on their clients' awards or settlements. Since going to trial is expensive and uncertain, settling out of court is often an attractive option for the lawyer. Attorneys may consciously believe that settling is in their clients' best interests. But how can they be objective, unbiased judges under these circumstances?

Research done with brokerage house analysts demonstrates how conflict of interest can unconsciously distort decision making. A survey of analysts conducted by the financial research service First Call showed that during a period in 2000 when the Nasdaq dropped 60%, fully 99% of brokerage analysts' client recommendations remained "strong buy," "buy," or "hold." What accounts for this discrepancy between what was happening and what was recommended? The answer may lie in a system that fosters conflicts of interest. A portion of analysts' pay is based on brokerage firm revenues. Some firms even tie analysts' compensation to the amount of business the analysts bring in from clients, giving analysts an obvious incentive to prolong and extend their relationships with clients. But to assume that during this Nasdaq free fall all brokerage house analysts were consciously corrupt, milking their clients to exploit this incentive system, defies common sense. Surely there were some bad apples. But how much more likely it is that most of these analysts believed their recommendations were sound and in their clients' best interests. What many didn't appreciate was that the built-in conflict of interest in their compensation incentives made it impossible for them to see the implicit bias in their own flawed recommendations.

Trying Harder Isn't Enough

As companies keep collapsing into financial scandal and ruin, corporations are responding with ethics-training programs for managers, and many of the world's leading business schools have created new courses and chaired professorships in ethics. Many of these efforts focus on teaching broad principles of moral philosophy to help managers understand the ethical challenges they face.

We applaud these efforts, but we doubt that a well-intentioned, just-try-harder approach will fundamentally improve the quality of executives' decision making. To do that, ethics training must be broadened to include what is now known about how our minds work and must expose managers directly to the unconscious mechanisms that underlie biased decision making. And it must provide managers with exercises and interventions that can root out the biases that lead to bad decisions.

Managers can make wiser, more ethical decisions if they become mindful of their unconscious biases. But how can we get at something outside our conscious awareness? By bringing the conscious mind to bear. Just as the driver of a misaligned car deliberately counteracts its pull, so can managers develop conscious strategies to counteract the pull of their unconscious biases. What's required is vigilance—continual awareness of the forces that can cause decision making to veer from its intended course and continual adjustments to counteract them. Those adjustments fall into three general categories: collecting data, shaping the environment, and broadening the decision-making process.

Collect data

The first step to reducing unconscious bias is to collect data to reveal its presence. Often, the data will be counterintuitive. Consider many people's surprise to learn of their own gender and racial biases on the IAT. Why the surprise? Because most of us trust the "statistics" our intuition provides. Better data are easily, but rarely, collected. One way to get those data is to examine our decisions in a systematic way.

Remember the MBA study groups whose participants overestimated their individual contributions to the group effort so that the totals averaged 139%? When the researchers asked group members to estimate what each of the other members' contributions were *before* claiming their own, the total fell to 121%. The tendency to claim too much credit still persisted, but this strategy of "unpacking" the work reduced the magnitude of the bias. In environments characterized by "I deserve more than you're giving me" claims, merely asking team members to unpack the contributions of others before claiming their own share of the pot usually aligns claims more closely with what's actually deserved. As this example demonstrates, such systematic audits of both individual and group decision-making processes can occur even as the decisions are being made.

Unpacking is a simple strategy that managers should routinely use to evaluate the fairness of their own claims within the organization. But they can also apply it in any situation where team members or subordinates may be overclaiming. For example, in explaining a raise that an employee feels is inadequate, a manager should ask the subordinate not what he thinks he alone deserves but what he considers an appropriate raise after taking into account each coworker's contribution and the pool available for pay increases. Similarly, when an individual feels she's doing more than her fair share of a team's work, asking her to consider other people's efforts before estimating her own can help align her perception with reality, restore her commitment, and reduce a skewed sense of entitlement.

Taking the IAT is another valuable strategy for collecting data. We recommend that you and others in your organization use the test to expose your own implicit biases. But one word of warning: Because the test is an educational and research tool, not a selection or evaluation tool, it is critical that you consider your results and others' to be private information. Simply knowing the magnitude and pervasiveness of your own biases can help direct your attention to areas of decision making that are in need of careful examination and reconsideration. For example, a manager whose testing reveals a bias toward certain groups ought to examine her hiring practices to see if she has indeed been disproportionately favoring those groups. But because so many people harbor such biases, they can also be generally acknowledged, and that knowledge can be used as the basis for changing the way decisions are made. It is important to guard against using pervasiveness to justify complacency and inaction: Pervasiveness of bias is not a mark of its appropriateness any more than poor eyesight is considered so ordinary a condition that it does not require corrective lenses.

Shape your environment

Research shows that implicit attitudes can be shaped by external cues in the environment. For example, Curtis Hardin and colleagues at UCLA used the IAT to study whether subjects' implicit race bias would be affected if the test was administered by a black investigator. One group of students took the test under the guidance of a white experimenter; another group took the test with a black experimenter. The mere presence of a black experimenter, Hardin found, reduced the level of subjects' implicit antiblack bias on the IAT. Numerous similar studies have shown similar effects with other social groups. What accounts for such shifts? We can speculate that experimenters in classrooms are assumed to be competent, in charge, and authoritative. Subjects guided by a black experimenter attribute these positive characteristics to that person, and then perhaps to the group as a whole. These findings suggest that one remedy for implicit bias is to expose oneself to images and social environments that challenge stereotypes.

We know of a judge whose court is located in a predominantly African-American neighborhood. Because of the crime and arrest patterns in the community, most people the judge sentences are black. The judge confronted a paradox. On the one hand, she took a judicial oath to be objective and egalitarian, and indeed she consciously believed that her decisions were unbiased. On the other hand, every day she was exposed to an environment that reinforced the association between black men and crime. Although she consciously rejected racial stereotypes, she suspected that she harbored unconscious prejudices merely from working in a segregated world. Immersed in this environment each day, she wondered if it was possible to give the defendants a fair hearing.

Rather than allow her environment to reinforce a bias, the judge created an alternative environment. She spent a vacation week sitting in a fellow judge's court in a neighborhood where the criminals being tried were predominantly white. Case after case challenged the stereotype of blacks as criminal and whites as law abiding and so challenged any bias against blacks that she might have harbored.

Think about the possibly biased associations your workplace fosters. Is there, perhaps, a "wall of fame" with pictures of high achievers all cast from the same mold? Are certain types of managers invariably promoted? Do people overuse certain analogies drawn from stereotypical or narrow domains of knowledge (sports metaphors, for instance, or cooking terms)? Managers can audit their organization to uncover such patterns or cues that unwittingly lead to stereotypical associations.

If an audit reveals that the environment may be promoting unconscious biased or unethical behavior, consider creating countervailing experiences, as the judge did. For example, if your department reinforces the stereotype of men as naturally dominant in a hierarchy (most managers are male, and most assistants are female), find a department with women in leadership positions and set up a shadow program. Both groups will benefit from the exchange of best practices, and your group will be quietly exposed to counterstereotypical cues. Managers sending people out to spend time in clients' organizations as a way to improve service should take care to select organizations likely to counter stereotypes reinforced in your own company.

Broaden your decision making

Imagine that you are making a decision in a meeting about an important company policy that will benefit some groups of employees more than others. A policy might, for example, provide extra vacation time for all employees but eliminate the flex time that has allowed many new parents to balance work with their family responsibilities. Another policy might lower the mandatory retirement age, eliminating some older workers but creating advancement opportunities for younger ones. Now pretend that, as you make your decisions, you don't know which group you belong to. That is, you don't know whether you are senior or junior, married or single, gay or straight, a parent or childless, male or female, healthy or unhealthy. You will eventually find out, but not until after the decision has been made. In this hypothetical scenario, what decision would you make? Would you be willing to risk being in the group disadvantaged by your own decision? How would your decisions differ if you could make them wearing various identities not your own?

This thought experiment is a version of philosopher John Rawls's concept of the "veil of ignorance," which posits that only a person ignorant of his own identity is capable of a truly ethical decision. Few of us can assume the veil completely, which is precisely why hidden biases, even when identified, are so difficult to correct. Still, applying the veil of ignorance to your next important managerial decision may offer some insight into how strongly implicit biases influence you.

Just as managers can expose bias by collecting data before acting on intuition, they can take other preemptive steps. What list of names do you start with when considering whom to send to a training program, recommend for a new assignment, or nominate for a fast-track position? Most of us can quickly and with little concentration come up with such a list. But keep in mind that your intuition is prone to implicit prejudice (which will strongly favor dominant and well-liked groups), in-group favoritism (which will favor people in your own group), overclaiming (which will favor you), and conflict of interest (which will favor people whose interests affect your own). Instead of relying on a mental short list when making personnel decisions, start with a full list of names of employees who have relevant qualifications.

Using a broad list of names has several advantages. The most obvious is that talent may surface that might otherwise be overlooked. Less obvious but equally important, the very act of considering a counterstereotypical choice at the conscious level can reduce implicit bias. In fact, merely thinking about hypothetical, counterstereotypical scenarios—such as what it would be like to trust a complex presentation to a female colleague or to receive a promotion from an African-American boss—can prompt less-biased and more ethical decision making. Similarly, consciously considering counterintuitive options in the face of conflicts of interest, or when there's an opportunity to overclaim, can promote more objective and ethical decisions.

The Vigilant Manager

If you answered "true" to the question at the start of this article, you felt with some confidence that you are an ethical decision maker. How would you answer it now? It's clear that neither simple conviction nor sincere intention is enough to ensure that you are the ethical practitioner you imagine yourself to be. Managers who aspire to be ethical must challenge the assumption that they're always unbiased and acknowledge that vigilance, even more than good intention, is a defining characteristic of an ethical manager. They must actively collect data, shape their environments, and broaden their decision making. What's more, an obvious redress is available. Managers should seek every opportunity to implement affirmative action policies—not because of past wrongs done to one group or another but because of the everyday wrongs that we can now document are inherent in the ordinary, everyday behavior of good, well-intentioned people. Ironically, only those who understand their own potential for unethical behavior can become the ethical decision makers that they aspire to be.

Originally published in December 2003. Reprint 5526.

The Discipline of Teams

by Jon R. Katzenbach and Douglas K. Smith

EARLY IN THE 1980S, Bill Greenwood and a small band of rebel railroaders took on most of the top management of Burlington Northern and created a multibillion-dollar business in "piggybacking" rail services despite widespread resistance, even resentment, within the company. The Medical Products Group at Hewlett-Packard owes most of its leading performance to the remarkable efforts of Dean Morton, Lew Platt, Ben Holmes, Dick Alberding, and a handful of their colleagues who revitalized a health care business that most others had written off. At Knight Ridder, Jim Batten's "customer obsession" vision took root at the *Tallahassee Democrat* when 14 frontline enthusiasts turned a charter to eliminate errors into a mission of major change and took the entire paper along with them.

Such are the stories and the work of teams—real teams that perform, not amorphous groups that we call teams because we think that the label is motivating and energizing. The difference between teams that perform and other groups that don't is a subject to which most of us pay far too little attention. Part of the problem is that "team" is a word and concept so familiar to everyone. (See "Not All Groups Are Teams: How to Tell the Difference.")

Or at least that's what we thought when we set out to do research for our book *The Wisdom of Teams* (HarperBusiness, 1993). We wanted to discover what differentiates various levels of team performance, where and how teams work best, and what top management can do to enhance their effectiveness. We talked with hundreds of people on more than 50 different teams in 30 companies and beyond, from Motorola and Hewlett-Packard to Operation Desert Storm and the Girl Scouts.

We found that there is a basic discipline that makes teams work. We also found that teams and good performance are inseparable: You cannot have one without the other. But people use the word "team" so loosely that it gets in the way of learning and applying the discipline that leads to good performance. For managers to make better decisions about whether, when, or how to encourage and use teams, it is important to be more precise about what a team is and what it isn't.

Most executives advocate teamwork. And they should. Teamwork represents a set of values that encourage listening and responding constructively to views expressed by others, giving others the benefit of the doubt, providing support, and recognizing the interests and achievements of others. Such values help teams perform, and they also promote individual performance as well as the performance of an entire organization. But teamwork values by themselves are not exclusive to teams, nor are they enough to ensure team performance. (See "Building Team Performance.")

Nor is a team just any group working together. Committees, councils, and task forces are not necessarily teams. Groups do not become teams simply because that is what someone calls them. The entire workforce of any large and complex organization is *never* a team, but think about how often that platitude is offered up.

To understand how teams deliver extra performance, we must distinguish between teams and other forms of working groups. That distinction turns on performance results. A working group's performance is a function of what its members do as individuals. A team's performance includes both individual results and what we call "collective work products." A collective work product is what two or more members must work on together, such as interviews, surveys, or experiments. Whatever it is, a collective work product reflects the joint, real contribution of team members.

Idea in Brief

The word *team* gets bandied about so loosely that many managers are oblivious to its real meaning—or its true potential. With a run-of-the-mill working group, performance is a function of what the members do as individuals. A team's performance, by contrast, calls for both individual and mutual accountability.

Though it may not seem like anything special, mutual accountability can lead to astonishing results. It enables a team to achieve performance levels that are far greater than the individual bests of the team's members. To achieve these benefits, team members must do more than listen, respond constructively, and provide support to one another. In addition to sharing these team-building values, they must share an essential *discipline*.

Working groups are both prevalent and effective in large organizations where individual accountability is most important. The best working groups come together to share information, perspectives, and insights; to make decisions that help each person do his or her job better; and to reinforce individual performance standards. But the focus is always on individual goals and accountabilities. Working-group members don't take responsibility for results other than their own. Nor do they try to develop incremental performance contributions requiring the combined work of two or more members.

Teams differ fundamentally from working groups because they require both individual and mutual accountability. Teams rely on more than group discussion, debate, and decision, on more than sharing information and best-practice performance standards. Teams produce discrete work products through the joint contributions of their members. This is what makes possible performance levels greater than the sum of all the individual bests of team members. Simply stated, a team is more than the sum of its parts.

The first step in developing a disciplined approach to team management is to think about teams as discrete units of performance and not just as positive sets of values. Having observed and worked with scores of teams in action, both successes and failures, we offer the following. Think of it as a working definition or, better still, an

Idea in Practice

A team's essential discipline comprises five characteristics:

1. **A meaningful common purpose that the team has helped shape.** Most teams are responding to an initial mandate from outside the team. But to be successful, the team must "own" this purpose, develop its own spin on it.

2. **Specific performance goals that flow from the common purpose.** For example, getting a new product to market in less than half the normal time. Compelling goals inspire and challenge a team, give it a sense of urgency. They also have a leveling effect, requiring members to focus on the collective effort necessary rather than any differences in title or status.

3. **A mix of complementary skills.** These include technical or functional expertise, problem-solving and decision-making skills, and interpersonal skills. Successful teams rarely have all the needed skills at the outset—they develop them as they learn what the challenge requires.

4. **A strong commitment to how the work gets done.** Teams must agree on who will do what jobs, how schedules will be established and honored, and how decisions will be made and modified. On a genuine team, each member does equivalent amounts of real work; all members, the leader included, contribute in concrete ways to the team's collective work-products.

essential discipline that real teams share: *A team is a small number of people with complementary skills who are committed to a common purpose, set of performance goals, and approach for which they hold themselves mutually accountable.*

The essence of a team is common commitment. Without it, groups perform as individuals; with it, they become a powerful unit of collective performance. This kind of commitment requires a purpose in which team members can believe. Whether the purpose is to "transform the contributions of suppliers into the satisfaction of customers," to "make our company one we can be proud of again," or to "prove that all children can learn," credible team purposes have an element related to winning, being first, revolutionizing, or being on the cutting edge.

5. **Mutual accountability.** Trust and commitment cannot be coerced. The process of agreeing upon appropriate goals serves as the crucible in which members forge their accountability to each other—not just to the leader.

Once the essential discipline has been established, a team is free to concentrate on the critical challenges it faces:

- For a team whose purpose is to make recommendations, that means making a fast and constructive start and providing a clean handoff to those who will implement the recommendations.

- For a team that makes or does things, it's keeping the specific performance goals in sharp focus.

- For a team that runs things, the primary task is distinguishing the challenges that require a real team approach from those that don't.

If a task doesn't demand joint work-products, a working group can be the more effective option. Team opportunities are usually those in which hierarchy or organizational boundaries inhibit the skills and perspectives needed for optimal results. Little wonder, then, that teams have become the primary units of productivity in high-performance organizations.

Teams develop direction, momentum, and commitment by working to shape a meaningful purpose. Building ownership and commitment to team purpose, however, is not incompatible with taking initial direction from outside the team. The often-asserted assumption that a team cannot "own" its purpose unless management leaves it alone actually confuses more potential teams than it helps. In fact, it is the exceptional case—for example, entrepreneurial situations—when a team creates a purpose entirely on its own.

Most successful teams shape their purposes in response to a demand or opportunity put in their path, usually by higher management. This helps teams get started by broadly framing the company's performance expectation. Management is responsible for clarifying the charter, rationale, and performance challenge for the team, but management must also leave enough flexibility for the team to develop commitment around its own spin on that purpose, set of specific goals, timing, and approach.

The best teams invest a tremendous amount of time and effort exploring, shaping, and agreeing on a purpose that belongs to them both collectively and individually. This "purposing" activity continues throughout the life of the team. By contrast, failed teams rarely develop a common purpose. For whatever reason—an insufficient focus on performance, lack of effort, poor leadership—they do not coalesce around a challenging aspiration.

The best teams also translate their common purpose into specific performance goals, such as reducing the reject rate from suppliers by 50% or increasing the math scores of graduates from 40% to 95%. Indeed, if a team fails to establish specific performance goals or if those goals do not relate directly to the team's overall purpose, team members become confused, pull apart, and revert to mediocre performance. By contrast, when purposes and goals build on one another and are combined with team commitment, they become a powerful engine of performance.

Transforming broad directives into specific and measurable performance goals is the surest first step for a team trying to shape a purpose meaningful to its members. Specific goals, such as getting a new product to market in less than half the normal time, responding to all customers within 24 hours, or achieving a zero-defect rate while simultaneously cutting costs by 40%, all provide firm footholds for teams. There are several reasons:

- Specific team-performance goals help define a set of work products that are different both from an organization-wide mission and from individual job objectives. As a result, such work products require the collective effort of team members to make something specific happen that, in and of itself, adds real value to results. By contrast, simply gathering from time to time to make decisions will not sustain team performance.

- The specificity of performance objectives facilitates clear communication and constructive conflict within the team.

When a plant-level team, for example, sets a goal of reducing average machine changeover time to two hours, the clarity of the goal forces the team to concentrate on what it would take either to achieve or to reconsider the goal. When such goals are clear, discussions can focus on how to pursue them or whether to change them; when goals are ambiguous or nonexistent, such discussions are much less productive.

- The attainability of specific goals helps teams maintain their focus on getting results. A product-development team at Eli Lilly's Peripheral Systems Division set definite yardsticks for the market introduction of an ultrasonic probe to help doctors locate deep veins and arteries.

  The probe had to have an audible signal through a specified depth of tissue, be capable of being manufactured at a rate of 100 per day, and have a unit cost less than a preestablished amount. Because the team could measure its progress against each of these specific objectives, the team knew throughout the development process where it stood. Either it had achieved its goals or not.

- As Outward Bound and other team-building programs illustrate, specific objectives have a leveling effect conducive to team behavior. When a small group of people challenge themselves to get over a wall or to reduce cycle time by 50%, their respective titles, perks, and other stripes fade into the background. The teams that succeed evaluate what and how each individual can best contribute to the team's goal and, more important, do so in terms of the performance objective itself rather than a person's status or personality.

- Specific goals allow a team to achieve small wins as it pursues its broader purpose. These small wins are invaluable to building commitment and overcoming the inevitable obstacles that get in the way of a long-term purpose. For example, the Knight Ridder team mentioned at the outset turned a narrow goal to eliminate errors into a compelling customer service purpose.

- Performance goals are compelling. They are symbols of accomplishment that motivate and energize. They challenge the people on a team to commit themselves, as a team, to make a difference. Drama, urgency, and a healthy fear of failure combine to drive teams that have their collective eye on an attainable, but challenging, goal. Nobody but the team can make it happen. It's their challenge.

The combination of purpose and specific goals is essential to performance. Each depends on the other to remain relevant and vital. Clear performance goals help a team keep track of progress and hold itself accountable; the broader, even nobler, aspirations in a team's purpose supply both meaning and emotional energy.

Virtually all effective teams we have met, read or heard about, or been members of have ranged between two and 25 people. For example, the Burlington Northern piggybacking team had seven members, and the Knight Ridder newspaper team had 14. The majority of them have numbered less than ten. Small size is admittedly more of a pragmatic guide than an absolute necessity for success. A large number of people, say 50 or more, can theoretically become a team. But groups of such size are more likely to break into subteams rather than function as a single unit.

Why? Large numbers of people have trouble interacting constructively as a group, much less doing real work together. Ten people are far more likely than 50 to work through their individual, functional, and hierarchical differences toward a common plan and to hold themselves jointly accountable for the results.

Large groups also face logistical issues, such as finding enough physical space and time to meet. And they confront more complex constraints, like crowd or herd behaviors, which prevent the intense sharing of viewpoints needed to build a team. As a result, when they try to develop a common purpose, they usually produce only superficial "missions" and well-meaning intentions that cannot be translated into concrete objectives. They tend fairly quickly to reach a point when meetings become a chore, a clear sign that most of the people in the group are uncertain why they have gathered, beyond some notion of getting along better. Anyone who has been through one of these exercises understands how frustrating it can be. This kind of failure tends to foster cynicism, which gets in the way of future team efforts.

In addition to finding the right size, teams must develop the right mix of skills; that is, each of the complementary skills necessary to do the team's job. As obvious as it sounds, it is a common failing in potential teams. Skill requirements fall into three fairly self-evident categories.

Technical or functional expertise

It would make little sense for a group of doctors to litigate an employment discrimination case in a court of law. Yet teams of doctors and lawyers often try medical malpractice or personal injury cases. Similarly, product development groups that include only marketers or engineers are less likely to succeed than those with the complementary skills of both.

Problem-solving and decision-making skills

Teams must be able to identify the problems and opportunities they face, evaluate the options they have for moving forward, and then make necessary trade-offs and decisions about how to proceed. Most teams need some members with these skills to begin with, although many will develop them best on the job.

Interpersonal skills

Common understanding and purpose cannot arise without effective communication and constructive conflict, which in turn depend on interpersonal skills. These skills include risk taking, helpful criticism, objectivity, active listening, giving the benefit of the doubt, and recognizing the interests and achievements of others.

Obviously, a team cannot get started without some minimum complement of skills, especially technical and functional ones. Still, think about how often you've been part of a team whose members were chosen primarily on the basis of personal compatibility or

Not All Groups Are Teams: How to Tell the Difference

Working Group
- Strong, clearly focused leader
- Individual accountability
- The group's purpose is the same as the broader organizational mission
- Individual work products
- Runs efficient meetings
- Measures its effectiveness indirectly by its influence on others (such as financial performance of the business)
- Discusses, decides, and delegates

Team
- Shared leadership roles
- Individual and mutual accountability
- Specific team purpose that the team itself delivers
- Collective work products
- Encourages open-ended discussion and active problem-solving meetings
- Measures performance directly by assessing collective work products
- Discusses, decides, and does real work together

formal position in the organization, and in which the skill mix of its members wasn't given much thought.

It is equally common to overemphasize skills in team selection. Yet in all the successful teams we've encountered, not one had all the needed skills at the outset. The Burlington Northern team, for example, initially had no members who were skilled marketers despite the fact that their performance challenge was a marketing one. In fact, we discovered that teams are powerful vehicles for developing the skills needed to meet the team's performance challenge.

Accordingly, team member selection ought to ride as much on skill potential as on skills already proven.

Effective teams develop strong commitment to a common approach; that is, to how they will work together to accomplish their purpose. Team members must agree on who will do particular jobs, how schedules will be set and adhered to, what skills need to be developed, how continuing membership in the team is to be earned, and how the group will make and modify decisions. This element of commitment is as important to team performance as the team's commitment to its purpose and goals.

Agreeing on the specifics of work and how they fit together to integrate individual skills and advance team performance lies at the heart of shaping a common approach. It is perhaps self-evident that an approach that delegates all the real work to a few members (or staff outsiders) and thus relies on reviews and meetings for its only "work together" aspects, cannot sustain a real team. Every member of a successful team does equivalent amounts of real work; all members, including the team leader, contribute in concrete ways to the team's work product. This is a very important element of the emotional logic that drives team performance.

When individuals approach a team situation, especially in a business setting, each has preexisting job assignments as well as strengths and weaknesses reflecting a variety of talents, backgrounds, personalities, and prejudices. Only through the mutual discovery and understanding of how to apply all its human resources to a common purpose can a team develop and agree on the best approach to achieve its goals. At the heart of such long and, at times, difficult interactions lies a commitment-building process in which the team candidly explores who is best suited to each task as well as how individual roles will come together. In effect, the team establishes a social contract among members that relates to their purpose and guides and obligates how they must work together.

No group ever becomes a team until it can hold itself accountable as a team. Like common purpose and approach, mutual accountability is a stiff test. Think, for example, about the subtle but critical difference between "the boss holds me accountable" and "we hold ourselves accountable." The first case can lead to the second, but without the second, there can be no team.

Companies like Hewlett-Packard and Motorola have an ingrained performance ethic that enables teams to form organically whenever there is a clear performance challenge requiring collective rather than individual effort. In these companies, the factor of mutual accountability is commonplace. "Being in the boat together" is how their performance game is played.

At its core, team accountability is about the sincere promises we make to ourselves and others, promises that underpin two critical aspects of effective teams: commitment and trust. Most of us enter a potential team situation cautiously because ingrained individualism and experience discourage us from putting our fates in the hands of others or accepting responsibility for others. Teams do not succeed by ignoring or wishing away such behavior.

Mutual accountability cannot be coerced any more than people can be made to trust one another. But when a team shares a common purpose, goals, and approach, mutual accountability grows as a natural counterpart. Accountability arises from and reinforces the time, energy, and action invested in figuring out what the team is trying to accomplish and how best to get it done.

When people work together toward a common objective, trust and commitment follow. Consequently, teams enjoying a strong common purpose and approach inevitably hold themselves responsible, both as individuals and as a team, for the team's performance. This sense of mutual accountability also produces the rich rewards of mutual achievement in which all members share. What we heard over and over from members of effective teams is that they found the experience energizing and motivating in ways that their "normal" jobs never could match.

On the other hand, groups established primarily for the sake of becoming a team or for job enhancement, communication, organizational effectiveness, or excellence rarely become effective teams, as demonstrated by the bad feelings left in many companies after experimenting with quality circles that never translated "quality" into specific goals. Only when appropriate performance goals are set does the process of discussing the goals and the approaches to them give team members a clearer and clearer choice: They can disagree with a goal and the path that the team selects and, in effect, opt out, or they can pitch in and become accountable with and to their teammates.

The discipline of teams we've outlined is critical to the success of all teams. Yet it is also useful to go one step further. Most teams can be classified in one of three ways: teams that recommend things, teams that make or do things, and teams that run things. In our experience, each type faces a characteristic set of challenges.

Teams that recommend things

These teams include task forces; project groups; and audit, quality, or safety groups asked to study and solve particular problems. Teams that recommend things almost always have predetermined completion dates. Two critical issues are unique to such teams: getting off to a fast and constructive start and dealing with the ultimate handoff that's required to get recommendations implemented.

The key to the first issue lies in the clarity of the team's charter and the composition of its membership. In addition to wanting to know why and how their efforts are important, task forces need a clear definition of whom management expects to participate and the time commitment required. Management can help by ensuring that the team includes people with the skills and influence necessary for crafting practical recommendations that will carry weight throughout the organization. Moreover, management can help the team get the necessary cooperation by opening doors and dealing with political obstacles.

Missing the handoff is almost always the problem that stymies teams that recommend things. To avoid this, the transfer of responsibility for recommendations to those who must implement them demands top management's time and attention. The more top managers assume that recommendations will "just happen," the less likely it is that they will. The more involvement task force members have in implementing their recommendations, the more likely they are to get implemented.

To the extent that people outside the task force will have to carry the ball, it is critical to involve them in the process early and often, certainly well before recommendations are finalized. Such involvement may take many forms, including participating in interviews, helping with analyses, contributing and critiquing ideas, and conducting experiments and trials. At a minimum, anyone responsible for implementation should receive a briefing on the task force's purpose, approach, and objectives at the beginning of the effort as well as regular reviews of progress.

Teams that make or do things

These teams include people at or near the front lines who are responsible for doing the basic manufacturing, development, operations, marketing, sales, service, and other value-adding activities of a business. With some exceptions, such as new-product development or process design teams, teams that make or do things tend to have no set completion dates because their activities are ongoing.

In deciding where team performance might have the greatest impact, top management should concentrate on what we call the company's "critical delivery points"—that is, places in the organization where the cost and value of the company's products and services are most directly determined. Such critical delivery points might include where accounts get managed, customer service performed, products designed, and productivity determined. If performance at critical delivery points depends on combining multiple skills, perspectives, and judgments in real time, then the team option is the smartest one.

When an organization does require a significant number of teams at these points, the sheer challenge of maximizing the performance of so many groups will demand a carefully constructed and performance-focused set of management processes. The issue here for top management is how to build the necessary systems and process supports without falling into the trap of appearing to promote teams for their own sake.

The imperative here, returning to our earlier discussion of the basic discipline of teams, is a relentless focus on performance. If management fails to pay persistent attention to the link between teams and performance, the organization becomes convinced that "this year, we are doing 'teams'." Top management can help by instituting processes like pay schemes and training for teams responsive to their real time needs, but more than anything else, top management must make clear and compelling demands on the teams themselves and then pay constant attention to their progress with respect to both team basics and performance results. This means focusing on specific teams and specific performance challenges. Otherwise "performance," like "team," will become a cliché.

Teams that run things

Despite the fact that many leaders refer to the group reporting to them as a team, few groups really are. And groups that become real teams seldom think of themselves as a team because they are so focused on performance results. Yet the opportunity for such teams includes groups from the top of the enterprise down through the divisional or functional level. Whether it is in charge of thousands of people or just a handful, as long as the group oversees some business, ongoing program, or significant functional activity, it is a team that runs things.

The main issue these teams face is determining whether a real team approach is the right one. Many groups that run things can be more effective as working groups than as teams. The key judgment is whether the sum of individual bests will suffice for the performance challenge at hand or whether the group must deliver substantial incremental performance requiring real joint work products. Although the team option promises greater performance, it also brings more risk, and managers must be brutally honest in assessing the trade-offs.

Members may have to overcome a natural reluctance to trust their fate to others. The price of faking the team approach is high: At best, members get diverted from their individual goals, costs outweigh benefits, and people resent the imposition on their time and priorities. At worst, serious animosities develop that undercut even the potential personal bests of the working-group approach.

Working groups present fewer risks. Effective working groups need little time to shape their purpose, since the leader usually establishes it. Meetings are run against well-prioritized agendas. And decisions are implemented through specific individual assignments and accountabilities. Most of the time, therefore, if performance aspirations can be met through individuals doing their respective jobs well, the working-group approach is more comfortable, less risky, and less disruptive than trying for more elusive team performance levels. Indeed, if there is no performance need for the team approach, efforts spent to improve the effectiveness of the working group make much more sense than floundering around trying to become a team.

Having said that, we believe the extra level of performance teams can achieve is becoming critical for a growing number of companies, especially as they move through major changes during which company performance depends on broad-based behavioral change. When top management uses teams to run things, it should make sure the team succeeds in identifying specific purposes and goals.

This is a second major issue for teams that run things. Too often, such teams confuse the broad mission of the total organization with the specific purpose of their small group at the top. The discipline of teams tells us that for a real team to form, there must be a team purpose that is distinctive and specific to the small group and that requires its members to roll up their sleeves and accomplish something beyond individual end products. If a group of managers looks only at the economic performance of the part of the organization it runs to assess overall effectiveness, the group will not have any team performance goals of its own.

While the basic discipline of teams does not differ for them, teams at the top are certainly the most difficult. The complexities of long-term challenges, heavy demands on executive time, and the deep-seated individualism of senior people conspire against teams at the top. At the same time, teams at the top are the most powerful. At first we thought such teams were nearly impossible. That is because we were looking at the teams as defined by the formal organizational structure; that is, the leader and all his or her direct reports equals the team. Then we discovered that real teams at the top were often smaller and less formalized: Whitehead and Weinberg at Goldman Sachs; Hewlett and Packard at HP; Krasnoff, Pall, and Hardy at Pall Corporation; Kendall, Pearson, and Calloway at Pepsi; Haas and Haas at Levi Strauss; Batten and Ridder at Knight Ridder. They were mostly twos and threes, with an occasional fourth.

Nonetheless, real teams at the top of large, complex organizations are still few and far between. Far too many groups at the top of large corporations needlessly constrain themselves from achieving real team levels of performance because they assume that all direct reports must be on the team, that team goals must be identical to corporate goals, that the team members' positions rather than skills determine their respective roles, that a team must be a team all the time, and that the team leader is above doing real work.

As understandable as these assumptions may be, most of them are unwarranted. They do not apply to the teams at the top we have observed, and when replaced with more realistic and flexible assumptions that permit the team discipline to be applied, real team performance at the top can and does occur. Moreover, as more and more companies are confronted with the need to manage major change across their organizations, we will see more real teams at the top.

We believe that teams will become the primary unit of performance in high-performance organizations. But that does not mean that teams will crowd out individual opportunity or formal hierarchy and process. Rather, teams will enhance existing structures without replacing them. A team opportunity exists anywhere hierarchy or organizational boundaries inhibit the skills and perspectives needed for optimal results. Thus, new-product innovation requires preserving functional excellence through structure while eradicating functional bias through teams. And frontline productivity requires preserving direction and guidance through hierarchy while drawing on energy and flexibility through self-managing teams.

We are convinced that every company faces specific performance challenges for which teams are the most practical and powerful vehicle at top management's disposal. The critical role for senior

Building Team Performance

Although there is no guaranteed how-to recipe for building team performance, we observed a number of approaches shared by many successful teams.

Establish urgency, demanding performance standards, and direction

All team members need to believe the team has urgent and worthwhile purposes, and they want to know what the expectations are. Indeed, the more urgent and meaningful the rationale, the more likely it is that the team will live up to its performance potential, as was the case for a customer-service team that was told that further growth for the entire company would be impossible without major improvements in that area. Teams work best in a compelling context. That is why companies with strong performance ethics usually form teams readily.

Select members for skill and skill potential, not personality

No team succeeds without all the skills needed to meet its purpose and performance goals. Yet most teams figure out the skills they will need after they are formed. The wise manager will choose people for their existing skills and their potential to improve existing skills and learn new ones.

Pay particular attention to first meetings and actions. Initial impressions always mean a great deal

When potential teams first gather, everyone monitors the signals given by others to confirm, suspend, or dispel assumptions and concerns. They pay particular attention to those in authority: the team leader and any executives who set up, oversee, or otherwise influence the team. And, as always, what such leaders do is more important than what they say. If a senior executive leaves the team kickoff to take a phone call ten minutes after the session has begun and he never returns, people get the message.

Set some clear rules of behavior

All effective teams develop rules of conduct at the outset to help them achieve their purpose and performance goals. The most critical initial rules pertain to attendance (for example, "no interruptions to take phone calls"), discussion ("no sacred cows"), confidentiality ("the only things to leave this room are what we agree on"), analytic approach ("facts are friendly"), end-product orientation ("everyone gets assignments and does them"), constructive confrontation ("no finger pointing"), and, often the most important, contributions ("everyone does real work").

Set and seize upon a few immediate performance-oriented tasks and goals

Most effective teams trace their advancement to key performance-oriented events. Such events can be set in motion by immediately establishing a few challenging goals that can be reached early on. There is no such thing as a real team without performance results, so the sooner such results occur, the sooner the team congeals.

Challenge the group regularly with fresh facts and information

New information causes a team to redefine and enrich its understanding of the performance challenge, thereby helping the team shape a common purpose, set clearer goals, and improve its common approach. A plant quality improvement team knew the cost of poor quality was high, but it wasn't until they researched the different types of defects and put a price tag on each one that they knew where to go next. Conversely, teams err when they assume that all the information needed exists in the collective experience and knowledge of their members.

Spend lots of time together

Common sense tells us that team members must spend a lot of time together, scheduled and unscheduled, especially in the beginning. Indeed, creative insights as well as personal bonding require impromptu and casual interactions just as much as analyzing spreadsheets and interviewing customers. Busy executives and managers too often intentionally minimize the time they spend together. The successful teams we've observed all gave themselves the time to learn to be a team. This time need not always be spent together physically; electronic, fax, and phone time can also count as time spent together.

Exploit the power of positive feedback, recognition, and reward

Positive reinforcement works as well in a team context as elsewhere. Giving out "gold stars" helps shape new behaviors critical to team performance. If people in the group, for example, are alert to a shy person's initial efforts to speak up and contribute, they can give the honest positive reinforcement that encourages continued contributions. There are many ways to recognize and reward team performance beyond direct compensation, from having a senior executive speak directly to the team about the urgency of its mission to using awards to recognize contributions. Ultimately, however, the satisfaction shared by a team in its own performance becomes the most cherished reward.

managers, therefore, is to worry about company performance and the kinds of teams that can deliver it. This means top management must recognize a team's unique potential to deliver results, deploy teams strategically when they are the best tool for the job, and foster the basic discipline of teams that will make them effective. By doing so, top management creates the kind of environment that enables team as well as individual and organizational performance.

Originally published in March 1993. Reprint R0507P.

Managing Your Boss

by John J. Gabarro and John P. Kotter

TO MANY PEOPLE, THE PHRASE "managing your boss" may sound unusual or suspicious. Because of the traditional top-down emphasis in most organizations, it is not obvious why you need to manage relationships upward—unless, of course, you would do so for personal or political reasons. But we are not referring to political maneuvering or to apple polishing. We are using the term to mean the process of consciously working with your superior to obtain the best possible results for you, your boss, and the company.

Recent studies suggest that effective managers take time and effort to manage not only relationships with their subordinates but also those with their bosses. These studies also show that this essential aspect of management is sometimes ignored by otherwise talented and aggressive managers. Indeed, some managers who actively and effectively supervise subordinates, products, markets, and technologies assume an almost passively reactive stance vis-à-vis their bosses. Such a stance almost always hurts them and their companies.

If you doubt the importance of managing your relationship with your boss or how difficult it is to do so effectively, consider for a moment the following sad but telling story:

Frank Gibbons was an acknowledged manufacturing genius in his industry and, by any profitability standard, a very effective executive. In 1973, his strengths propelled him into the position of vice president of manufacturing for the second largest and most profitable company in its industry. Gibbons was not, however, a good manager of people. He knew this, as did others in his company and his industry. Recognizing this weakness, the president made sure that those who reported to Gibbons were good at working with people and could compensate for his limitations. The arrangement worked well.

In 1975, Philip Bonnevie was promoted into a position reporting to Gibbons. In keeping with the previous pattern, the president selected Bonnevie because he had an excellent track record and a reputation for being good with people. In making that selection, however, the president neglected to notice that, in his rapid rise through the organization, Bonnevie had always had good-to-excellent bosses. He had never been forced to manage a relationship with a difficult boss. In retrospect, Bonnevie admits he had never thought that managing his boss was a part of his job.

Fourteen months after he started working for Gibbons, Bonnevie was fired. During that same quarter, the company reported a net loss for the first time in seven years. Many of those who were close to these events say that they don't really understand what happened. This much is known, however: While the company was bringing out a major new product—a process that required sales, engineering, and manufacturing groups to coordinate decisions very carefully—a whole series of misunderstandings and bad feelings developed between Gibbons and Bonnevie.

For example, Bonnevie claims Gibbons was aware of and had accepted Bonnevie's decision to use a new type of machinery to make the new product; Gibbons swears he did not. Furthermore, Gibbons claims he made it clear to Bonnevie that the introduction of the product was too important to the company in the short run to take any major risks.

As a result of such misunderstandings, planning went awry: A new manufacturing plant was built that could not produce the new product designed by engineering, in the volume desired by sales, at a cost agreed on by the executive committee. Gibbons blamed Bonnevie for the mistake. Bonnevie blamed Gibbons.

Idea in Brief

Managing our *bosses*? Isn't that merely manipulation? Corporate cozying up? Out-and-out apple polishing? In fact, we manage our bosses for very good reasons: to get resources to do the best job, not only for ourselves, but for our bosses and our companies as well. We actively pursue a healthy and productive working relationship based on mutual respect and understanding—understanding our own and our bosses' strengths, weaknesses, goals, work styles, and needs. Here's what can happen when we don't:

Example: A new president with a formal work style replaced someone who'd been looser, more intuitive. The new president preferred written reports and structured meetings. One of his managers found this too controlling. He seldom sent background information, and was often blindsided by unanticipated questions. His boss found their meetings inefficient and frustrating. The manager had to resign.

In contrast, here's how another manager's sensitivity to this same boss's style really paid off:

Example: This manager identified the kinds and frequency of information the president wanted. He sent ahead background reports and discussion agendas. The result? Highly productive meetings and even more innovative problem solving than with his previous boss.

Managers often don't realize how much their bosses depend on them. They need cooperation, reliability, and honesty from their direct reports. Many managers also don't realize how much *they* depend on their bosses—for links to the rest of the organization, for setting priorities, and for obtaining critical resources.

Recognizing this mutual dependence, effective managers seek out information about the boss's concerns and are sensitive to his work style. They also understand how their own attitudes toward authority can sabotage the relationship. Some see the boss as the enemy and fight him at every turn; others are overly compliant, viewing the boss as an all-wise parent.

Of course, one could argue that the problem here was caused by Gibbons's inability to manage his subordinates. But one can make just as strong a case that the problem was related to Bonnevie's inability to manage his boss. Remember, Gibbons was not having difficulty with any other subordinates. Moreover, given the personal

Idea in Practice

You can benefit from this mutual dependence and develop a very productive relationship with your boss by focusing on:

- **compatible work styles.** Bosses process information differently. "Listeners" prefer to be briefed in person so they can ask questions. "Readers" want to process written information first, and then meet to discuss.

  Decision-making styles also vary. Some bosses are highly involved. Touch base with them frequently. Others prefer to delegate. Inform them about important decisions you've already made.

- **mutual expectations.** Don't passively assume you know what the boss expects. Find out. With some bosses, write detailed outlines of your work for their approval. With others, carefully planned discussions are key.

Also, communicate *your* expectations to find out if they are realistic. Persuade the boss to accept the most important ones.

- **information flow.** Managers typically underestimate what their bosses need to know—and what they *do* know. Keep the boss informed through processes that fit his style. Be forthright about both good and bad news.

- **dependability and honesty.** Trustworthy subordinates only make promises they can keep and don't shade the truth or play down difficult issues.

- **good use of time and resources.** Don't waste your boss's time with trivial issues. Selectively draw on his time and resources to meet the most important goals—yours, his, and the company's.

price paid by Bonnevie (being fired and having his reputation within the industry severely tarnished), there was little consolation in saying the problem was that Gibbons was poor at managing subordinates. Everyone already knew that.

We believe that the situation could have turned out differently had Bonnevie been more adept at understanding Gibbons and at managing his relationship with him. In this case, an inability to manage upward was unusually costly. The company lost $2 million to $5 million, and Bonnevie's career was, at least temporarily, disrupted. Many less costly cases similar to this probably occur regularly in all major corporations, and the cumulative effect can be very destructive.

Misreading the Boss–Subordinate Relationship

People often dismiss stories like the one we just related as being merely cases of personality conflict. Because two people can on occasion be psychologically or temperamentally incapable of working together, this can be an apt description. But more often, we have found, a personality conflict is only a part of the problem—sometimes a very small part.

Bonnevie did not just have a different personality from Gibbons, he also made or had unrealistic assumptions and expectations about the very nature of boss–subordinate relationships. Specifically, he did not recognize that his relationship to Gibbons involved *mutual dependence* between two *fallible* human beings. Failing to recognize this, a manager typically either avoids trying to manage his or her relationship with a boss or manages it ineffectively.

Some people behave as if their bosses were not very dependent on them. They fail to see how much the boss needs their help and cooperation to do his or her job effectively. These people refuse to acknowledge that the boss can be severely hurt by their actions and needs cooperation, dependability, and honesty from them.

Some people see themselves as not very dependent on their bosses. They gloss over how much help and information they need from the boss in order to perform their own jobs well. This superficial view is particularly damaging when a manager's job and decisions affect other parts of the organization, as was the case in Bonnevie's situation. A manager's immediate boss can play a critical role in linking the manager to the rest of the organization, making sure the manager's priorities are consistent with organizational needs, and in securing the resources the manager needs to perform well. Yet some managers need to see themselves as practically self-sufficient, as not needing the critical information and resources a boss can supply.

Many managers, like Bonnevie, assume that the boss will magically know what information or help their subordinates need and provide it to them. Certainly, some bosses do an excellent job of caring for their subordinates in this way, but for a manager to expect that from all bosses is dangerously unrealistic. A more reasonable expectation for managers to have is that modest help will be forthcoming. After all, bosses are only human. Most really effective managers accept this fact and assume primary responsibility for their own careers and development. They make a point of seeking the information and help they need to do a job instead of waiting for their bosses to provide it.

In light of the foregoing, it seems to us that managing a situation of mutual dependence among fallible human beings requires the following:

1. You have a good understanding of the other person and yourself, especially regarding strengths, weaknesses, work styles, and needs.

2. You use this information to develop and manage a healthy working relationship—one that is compatible with both people's work styles and assets, is characterized by mutual expectations, and meets the most critical needs of the other person.

This combination is essentially what we have found highly effective managers doing.

Understanding the Boss

Managing your boss requires that you gain an understanding of the boss and his or her context, as well as your own situation. All managers do this to some degree, but many are not thorough enough.

At a minimum, you need to appreciate your boss's goals and pressures, his or her strengths and weaknesses. What are your boss's organizational and personal objectives, and what are his or her pressures, especially those from his or her own boss and others at the same level? What are your boss's long suits and blind spots?

What is the preferred style of working? Does your boss like to get information through memos, formal meetings, or phone calls? Does he or she thrive on conflict or try to minimize it? Without this information, a manager is flying blind when dealing with the boss, and unnecessary conflicts, misunderstandings, and problems are inevitable.

In one situation we studied, a top-notch marketing manager with a superior performance record was hired into a company as a vice president "to straighten out the marketing and sales problems." The company, which was having financial difficulties, had recently been acquired by a larger corporation. The president was eager to turn it around and gave the new marketing vice president free rein—at least initially. Based on his previous experience, the new vice president correctly diagnosed that greater market share was needed for the company and that strong product management was required to bring that about. Following that logic, he made a number of pricing decisions aimed at increasing high-volume business.

When margins declined and the financial situation did not improve, however, the president increased pressure on the new vice president. Believing that the situation would eventually correct itself as the company gained back market share, the vice president resisted the pressure.

When by the second quarter, margins and profits had still failed to improve, the president took direct control over all pricing decisions and put all items on a set level of margin, regardless of volume. The new vice president began to find himself shut out by the president, and their relationship deteriorated. In fact, the vice president found the president's behavior bizarre. Unfortunately, the president's new pricing scheme also failed to increase margins, and by the fourth quarter, both the president and the vice president were fired.

What the new vice president had not known until it was too late was that improving marketing and sales had been only *one* of the president's goals. His most immediate goal had been to make the company more profitable—quickly.

Nor had the new vice president known that his boss was invested in this short-term priority for personal as well as business reasons.

The president had been a strong advocate of the acquisition within the parent company, and his personal credibility was at stake.

The vice president made three basic errors. He took information supplied to him at face value, he made assumptions in areas where he had no information, and—what was most damaging—he never actively tried to clarify what his boss's objectives were. As a result, he ended up taking actions that were actually at odds with the president's priorities and objectives.

Managers who work effectively with their bosses do not behave this way. They seek out information about the boss's goals and problems and pressures. They are alert for opportunities to question the boss and others around him or her to test their assumptions. They pay attention to clues in the boss's behavior. Although it is imperative that they do this especially when they begin working with a new boss, effective managers also do this on an ongoing basis because they recognize that priorities and concerns change.

Being sensitive to a boss's work style can be crucial, especially when the boss is new. For example, a new president who was organized and formal in his approach replaced a man who was informal and intuitive. The new president worked best when he had written reports. He also preferred formal meetings with set agendas.

One of his division managers realized this need and worked with the new president to identify the kinds and frequency of information and reports that the president wanted. This manager also made a point of sending background information and brief agendas ahead of time for their discussions. He found that with this type of preparation their meetings were very useful. Another interesting result was, he found that with adequate preparation his new boss was even more effective at brainstorming problems than his more informal and intuitive predecessor had been.

In contrast, another division manager never fully understood how the new boss's work style differed from that of his predecessor. To the degree that he did sense it, he experienced it as too much control. As a result, he seldom sent the new president the background information he needed, and the president never felt fully prepared for meetings with the manager. In fact, the president spent much of the time when they met trying to get information that he felt he should have had earlier. The boss experienced these meetings as frustrating and inefficient, and the subordinate often found himself thrown off guard by the questions that the president asked. Ultimately, this division manager resigned.

The difference between the two division managers just described was not so much one of ability or even adaptability. Rather, one of the men was more sensitive to his boss's work style and to the implications of his boss's needs than the other was.

Understanding Yourself

The boss is only one-half of the relationship. You are the other half, as well as the part over which you have more direct control. Developing an effective working relationship requires, then, that you know your own needs, strengths and weaknesses, and personal style.

You are not going to change either your basic personality structure or that of your boss. But you can become aware of what it is about you that impedes or facilitates working with your boss and, with that awareness, take actions that make the relationship more effective.

For example, in one case we observed, a manager and his superior ran into problems whenever they disagreed. The boss's typical response was to harden his position and overstate it. The manager's reaction was then to raise the ante and intensify the forcefulness of his argument. In doing this, he channeled his anger into sharpening his attacks on the logical fallacies he saw in his boss's assumptions. His boss in turn would become even more adamant about holding his original position. Predictably, this escalating cycle resulted in the subordinate avoiding whenever possible any topic of potential conflict with his boss.

In discussing this problem with his peers, the manager discovered that his reaction to the boss was typical of how he generally reacted to counterarguments—but with a difference. His response would overwhelm his peers but not his boss. Because his attempts to discuss this problem with his boss were unsuccessful, he concluded that the only way to change the situation was to deal with his own instinctive reactions. Whenever the two reached an impasse, he would check his own impatience and suggest that they break up and think about it before getting together again. Usually when they renewed their discussion, they had digested their differences and were more able to work them through.

Gaining this level of self-awareness and acting on it are difficult but not impossible. For example, by reflecting over his past experiences, a young manager learned that he was not very good at dealing with difficult and emotional issues where people were involved. Because he disliked those issues and realized that his instinctive responses to them were seldom very good, he developed a habit of touching base with his boss whenever such a problem arose. Their discussions always surfaced ideas and approaches the manager had not considered. In many cases, they also identified specific actions the boss could take to help.

Although a superior–subordinate relationship is one of mutual dependence, it is also one in which the subordinate is typically more dependent on the boss than the other way around. This dependence inevitably results in the subordinate feeling a certain degree of frustration, sometimes anger, when his actions or options are constrained by his boss's decisions. This is a normal part of life and occurs in the best of relationships. The way in which a manager handles these frustrations largely depends on his or her predisposition toward dependence on authority figures.

Some people's instinctive reaction under these circumstances is to resent the boss's authority and to rebel against the boss's decisions. Sometimes a person will escalate a conflict beyond what is appropriate. Seeing the boss almost as an institutional enemy, this type of manager will often, without being conscious of it, fight with the boss just for the sake of fighting. The subordinate's reactions to being constrained are usually strong and sometimes impulsive. He or she sees the boss as someone who, by virtue of the role, is a hindrance to progress, an obstacle to be circumvented or at best tolerated.

Psychologists call this pattern of reactions counterdependent behavior. Although a counterdependent person is difficult for most superiors to manage and usually has a history of strained relationships with superiors, this sort of manager is apt to have even more trouble with a boss who tends to be directive or authoritarian. When the manager acts on his or her negative feelings, often in subtle and nonverbal ways, the boss sometimes does become the enemy. Sensing the subordinate's latent hostility, the boss will lose trust in the subordinate or his or her judgment and then behave even less openly.

Paradoxically, a manager with this type of predisposition is often a good manager of his or her own people. He or she will many times go out of the way to get support for them and will not hesitate to go to bat for them.

At the other extreme are managers who swallow their anger and behave in a very compliant fashion when the boss makes what they know to be a poor decision. These managers will agree with the boss even when a disagreement might be welcome or when the boss would easily alter a decision if given more information. Because they bear no relationship to the specific situation at hand, their responses are as much an overreaction as those of counterdependent managers. Instead of seeing the boss as an enemy, these people deny their anger—the other extreme—and tend to see the boss as if he or she were an all-wise parent who should know best, should take responsibility for their careers, train them in all they need to know, and protect them from overly ambitious peers.

Both counterdependence and overdependence lead managers to hold unrealistic views of what a boss is. Both views ignore that bosses, like everyone else, are imperfect and fallible. They don't have unlimited time, encyclopedic knowledge, or extrasensory perception; nor are they evil enemies. They have their own pressures and concerns that are sometimes at odds with the wishes of the subordinate—and often for good reason.

Altering predispositions toward authority, especially at the extremes, is almost impossible without intensive psychotherapy (psychoanalytic theory and research suggest that such predispositions are deeply rooted in a person's personality and upbringing).

However, an awareness of these extremes and the range between them can be very useful in understanding where your own predispositions fall and what the implications are for how you tend to behave in relation to your boss.

If you believe, on the one hand, that you have some tendencies toward counterdependence, you can understand and even predict what your reactions and overreactions are likely to be. If, on the other hand, you believe you have some tendencies toward overdependence, you might question the extent to which your overcompliance or inability to confront real differences may be making both you and your boss less effective.

Developing and Managing the Relationship

With a clear understanding of both your boss and yourself, you can *usually* establish a way of working together that fits both of you, that is characterized by unambiguous mutual expectations, and that

---

Checklist for Managing Your Boss

Make sure you understand your boss and his or her context, including:
- [ ] Goals and objectives
- [ ] Pressures
- [ ] Strengths, weaknesses, blind spots
- [ ] Preferred work style

Assess yourself and your needs, including:
- [ ] Strengths and weaknesses
- [ ] Personal style
- [ ] Predisposition toward dependence on authority figures

Develop and maintain a relationship that:
- [ ] Fits both your needs and styles
- [ ] Is characterized by mutual expectations
- [ ] Keeps your boss informed
- [ ] Is based on dependability and honesty
- [ ] Selectively uses your boss's time and resources

---

helps you both be more productive and effective. The "Checklist for managing your boss" summarizes some things such a relationship consists of. Following are a few more.

Compatible work styles

Above all else, a good working relationship with a boss accommodates differences in work style. For example, in one situation we studied, a manager (who had a relatively good relationship with his superior) realized that during meetings his boss would often become inattentive and sometimes brusque. The subordinate's own style tended to be discursive and exploratory. He would often digress from the topic at hand to deal with background factors, alternative approaches, and so forth. His boss preferred to discuss problems with a minimum of background detail and became impatient and distracted whenever his subordinate digressed from the immediate issue.

Recognizing this difference in style, the manager became terser and more direct during meetings with his boss. To help himself do this, before meetings, he would develop brief agendas that he used as a guide. Whenever he felt that a digression was needed, he explained why. This small shift in his own style made these meetings more effective and far less frustrating for both of them.

Subordinates can adjust their styles in response to their bosses' preferred method for receiving information. Peter Drucker divides bosses into "listeners" and "readers." Some bosses like to get information in report form so they can read and study it. Others work better with information and reports presented in person so they can ask questions. As Drucker points out, the implications are obvious. If your boss is a listener, you brief him or her in person, *then* follow it up with a memo. If your boss is a reader, you cover important items or proposals in a memo or report, *then* discuss them.

Other adjustments can be made according to a boss's decision-making style. Some bosses prefer to be involved in decisions and problems as they arise. These are high-involvement managers who like to keep their hands on the pulse of the operation. Usually their needs (and your own) are best satisfied if you touch base with them on an ad hoc basis. A boss who has a need to be involved will become involved one way or another, so there are advantages to including him or her at your initiative. Other bosses prefer to delegate—they don't want to be involved. They expect you to come to them with major problems and inform them about any important changes.

Creating a compatible relationship also involves drawing on each other's strengths and making up for each other's weaknesses. Because he knew that the boss—the vice president of engineering— was not very good at monitoring his employees' problems, one manager we studied made a point of doing it himself. The stakes were high: The engineers and technicians were all union members, the company worked on a customer-contract basis, and the company had recently experienced a serious strike.

The manager worked closely with his boss, along with people in the scheduling department and the personnel office, to make sure that potential problems were avoided. He also developed an informal arrangement through which his boss would review with him any proposed changes in personnel or assignment policies before taking action. The boss valued his advice and credited his subordinate for improving both the performance of the division and the labor–management climate.

Mutual expectations

The subordinate who passively assumes that he or she knows what the boss expects is in for trouble. Of course, some superiors will spell out their expectations very explicitly and in great detail. But most do not. And although many corporations have systems that provide a basis for communicating expectations (such as formal planning processes, career planning reviews, and performance appraisal reviews), these systems never work perfectly. Also, between these formal reviews, expectations invariably change.

Ultimately, the burden falls on the subordinate to find out what the boss's expectations are. They can be both broad (such as what kinds of problems the boss wishes to be informed about and when) as well as very specific (such things as when a particular project should be completed and what kinds of information the boss needs in the interim).

Getting a boss who tends to be vague or not explicit to express expectations can be difficult. But effective managers find ways to get that information. Some will draft a detailed memo covering key aspects of their work and then send it to their boss for approval. They then follow this up with a face-to-face discussion in which they go over each item in the memo. A discussion like this will often surface virtually all of the boss's expectations.

Other effective managers will deal with an inexplicit boss by initiating an ongoing series of informal discussions about "good management" and "our objectives." Still others find useful information more indirectly through those who used to work for the boss and through the formal planning systems in which the boss makes commitments to his or her own superior. Which approach you choose, of course, should depend on your understanding of your boss's style.

Developing a workable set of mutual expectations also requires that you communicate your own expectations to the boss, find out if they are realistic, and influence the boss to accept the ones that are important to you. Being able to influence the boss to value your expectations can be particularly important if the boss is an overachiever. Such a boss will often set unrealistically high standards that need to be brought into line with reality.

A flow of information

How much information a boss needs about what a subordinate is doing will vary significantly depending on the boss's style, the situation he or she is in, and the confidence the boss has in the subordinate. But it is not uncommon for a boss to need more information than the subordinate would naturally supply or for the subordinate to think the boss knows more than he or she really does. Effective managers recognize that they probably underestimate what their bosses need to know and make sure they find ways to keep them informed through processes that fit their styles.

Managing the flow of information upward is particularly difficult if the boss does not like to hear about problems. Although many people would deny it, bosses often give off signals that they want to hear only good news. They show great displeasure—usually nonverbally—when someone tells them about a problem. Ignoring individual achievement, they may even evaluate more favorably subordinates who do not bring problems to them.

Nevertheless, for the good of the organization, the boss, and the subordinate, a superior needs to hear about failures as well as successes. Some subordinates deal with a good-news-only boss by finding indirect ways to get the necessary information to him or her, such as a management information system. Others see to it that potential problems, whether in the form of good surprises or bad news, are communicated immediately.

Dependability and honesty

Few things are more disabling to a boss than a subordinate on whom he cannot depend, whose work he cannot trust. Almost no one is intentionally undependable, but many managers are inadvertently so because of oversight or uncertainty about the boss's priorities. A commitment to an optimistic delivery date may please a superior in the short term but become a source of displeasure if not honored. It's difficult for a boss to rely on a subordinate who repeatedly slips deadlines. As one president (describing a subordinate) put it: "I'd rather he be more consistent even if he delivered fewer peak successes—at least I could rely on him."

Nor are many managers intentionally dishonest with their bosses. But it is easy to shade the truth and play down issues. Current concerns often become future surprise problems. It's almost impossible for bosses to work effectively if they cannot rely on a fairly accurate reading from their subordinates. Because it undermines credibility, dishonesty is perhaps the most troubling trait a subordinate can have. Without a basic level of trust, a boss feels compelled to check all of a subordinate's decisions, which makes it difficult to delegate.

Good use of time and resources

Your boss is probably as limited in his or her store of time, energy, and influence as you are. Every request you make of your boss uses up some of these resources, so it's wise to draw on these resources selectively. This may sound obvious, but many managers use up their boss's time (and some of their own credibility) over relatively trivial issues.

One vice president went to great lengths to get his boss to fire a meddlesome secretary in another department. His boss had to use considerable influence to do it. Understandably, the head of the other department was not pleased. Later, when the vice president wanted to tackle more important problems, he ran into trouble. By using up blue chips on a relatively trivial issue, he had made it difficult for him and his boss to meet more important goals.

No doubt, some subordinates will resent that on top of all their other duties, they also need to take time and energy to manage their relationships with their bosses. Such managers fail to realize the importance of this activity and how it can simplify their jobs by eliminating potentially severe problems. Effective managers recognize that this part of their work is legitimate. Seeing themselves as ultimately responsible for what they achieve in an organization, they know they need to establish and manage relationships with everyone on whom they depend—and that includes the boss.

Originally published in January 1980. Reprint R0501J.

About the Contributors

DANIEL GOLEMAN cochairs the Consortium for Research on Emotional Intelligence in Organizations at Rutgers University.

FREDERICK HERZBERG was a professor of management at the University of Utah.

JEAN-FRANÇOIS MANZONI is a professor of leadership and organizational development at IMD in Switzerland.

JEAN-LOUIS BARSOUX is a senior research fellow at Insead in France.

CAROL A. WALKER is the president of Prepared to Lead, a management consulting firm in Weston, Massachusetts.

MARCUS BUCKINGHAM is a consultant and speaker on leadership and management practices.

W. CHAN KIM is the Boston Consulting Group Bruce D. Henderson Chaired Professor of Strategy and International Management at Insead in France.

RENÉE MAUBORGNE is the Insead Distinguished Fellow and a professor of strategy at Insead in France.

CHRIS ARGYRIS is a professor emeritus at Harvard's Graduate School of Education.

MAHZARIN R. BANAJI is the Richard Clarke Cabot Professor of Social Ethics at Harvard University.

MAX H. BAZERMAN is the Jesse Isidor Straus Professor of Business Administration at Harvard Business School.

DOLLY CHUGH is an assistant professor of management and organizations at New York University's Stern School of Business.

JON R. KATZENBACH is a senior partner at Booz & Company, a global management consulting firm.

DOUGLAS K. SMITH is an organizational consultant and a former McKinsey & Company partner.

JOHN J. GABARRO is the UPS Foundation Professor of Human Resource Management, Emeritus, at Harvard Business School.

JOHN P. KOTTER is the Konosuke Matsushita Professor of Leadership, Emeritus, at Harvard Business School.

Index

research on, 58
reversing, 54–55, 63–64
self-fulfilling and self-reinforcing
aspects of, 53, 65
shutting down by employees in,
60–61
start of, 52, 54, 56–57
steps in, 59
sexism, 158–159
Siemens-Nixdorf Informationssysteme (SNI), 118–119
single-loop learning, 134–135
size of teams, 182–183
skills, and team discipline, 178,
183–185, 192
Smith, Douglas K., 175–194
social awareness, and emotional
intelligence, 9
social skill
emotional intelligence and traits
of, 9
leadership styles and, 3
standards
authoritative leadership style
and, 11, 13
correlations between leadership
style and, 10
organizational climate and, 4
team performance and, 192
stereotypes
environmental cues and, 159, 161,
170–171
hiring decisions and, 161–162
implicit prejudice and, 158, 160,
162
strategic thinking, and new managers, 79, 81, 87–88, 90
strategy, and leadership, 1
strengths of employees, and great
managers, 93, 94–95, 102–105
Stringer, Richard, 4
support for new managers, 80,
82–84

Tallahassee Democrat, 175
task forces, 187–188
Taylor, Frederick Winslow, 125
Teaching Tolerance, 164
team-building programs, 181
teams, 175–194
building performance of, 192–193
challenges for, 179
characteristics of discipline of,
178–179
classification of, 187–191
commitment of, 178, 185
as discrete units of performance,
177–178
making or doing things by,
188–189
mutual accountability and, 178,
185–186
performance goals and, 178,
180–182
purpose of, 178, 179–180
recommendations from, 187–188
research on, 175–176
size of, 182–183
skills requirements of, 183–185
teams at the top and, 190–191
teams that run things, 189–191
working groups compared with,
176–177, 184, 189–190
Thibaut, John W., 117
Thomas v. Kodak, 162
time use, and managing your boss,
198, 210–211
Torre, Joe, 12–13
training
for employees, from great
managers, 104
in ethics, 158, 167–168
for new managers, 78
trust
fair process and, 112, 113, 114, 115,
116, 117–118, 120, 121, 123, 125,
126, 128, 130, 131

The most important management ideas all in one place.

We hope you enjoyed this book from *Harvard Business Review*. Now you can get even more with HBR's 10 Must Reads Boxed Set. From books on leadership and strategy to managing yourself and others, this 6-book collection delivers articles on the most essential business topics to help you succeed.

HBR's 10 Must Reads Series

The definitive collection of ideas and best practices on our most sought-after topics from the best minds in business.

- Change Management
- Collaboration
- Communication
- Emotional Intelligence
- Innovation
- Leadership
- Making Smart Decisions

- Managing Across Cultures
- Managing People
- Managing Yourself
- Strategic Marketing
- Strategy
- Teams
- The Essentials

hbr.org/mustreads